D0939012

New England Transcendentalism
and
St. Louis Hegelianism

New England Transcendentalism
AND
St. Louis Hegelianism

Phases in the History of American Idealism

BY

HENRY A. POCHMANN
Professor of English, University of Wisconsin

HASKELL HOUSE PUBLISHERS Ltd.
Publishers of Scarce Scholarly Books
NEW YORK. N. Y. 10012
1970

First Published 1948

HASKELL HOUSE PUBLISHERS Ltd.
Publishers of Scarce Scholarly Books
280 LAFAYETTE STREET
NEW YORK. N. Y. 10012

Library of Congress Catalog Card Number: 68-55163

Standard Book Number 8383-0610-1

Printed in the United States of America

NEW ENGLAND TRANSCENDENTALISM AND

ST. LOUIS HEGELIANISM

Phases in the History of American Idealism

THE OLD SAYING that "East is East and West is West, and never the twain shall meet" is often discredited; yet the whole of nineteenth-century American history is full of instances to show that the two, while mutually complementary, often clashed irreconcilably. Notable cases are the relations between New England Transcendentalism and the St. Louis Movement in Philosophy, Literature, and Education and, somewhat later, the interactions between the latter and the Concord School of Philosophy. Ralph Waldo Emerson and William Torrey Harris were the hierarchs of the two movements, ably supported, particularly in the philosophical pretensions of the movements, by Amos Bronson Alcott and Henry Conrad Brokmeyer, respectively. The near harmony between the related schools is best typified by the relations between Emerson and Harris; their conflict, by Alcott and Brokmeyer. The meeting of the last two is an exciting episode in the history of idealism in America. It was a joust in which Plato tilted against Hegel for supremacy over the West— for supremacy over the whole nation, as the St. Louisans, caught in their own expansionist optimism, saw it. The protagonists and the setting of this duel are in themselves matters of interest, no less than the duel itself.

I. THE HEGELIZATION OF THE WEST

Brokmeyer, a refugee from Prussian militarism, landed, a lad of sixteen, in New York in 1844 with twenty-five cents in his pocket, three English words in his vocabulary, and a stock of independent ideas. Bootblack, currier, tanner, shoemaker, and jack-of-all-trades, he pursued a vagrant way westward and as far south as Lowndes and Oktibbeha counties. Mississippi, where he amassed a small fortune operating a tannery and shoe factory, employing slave labor to manufacture shoes that cost him six and one-fourth cents (in Southern parlance, "a half-bit") a pair to make. Tiring of money-grubbing, and aspiring to supplement his practical experiences, he resumed his interrupted educational career by entering Georgetown University in Kentucky, and literally arguing his way into and out of several institutions of higher learning. At Brown University he engaged in especially joyous disputation with President Wayland, picking up by the way solid kernels of Emersonian idealism and seemingly all the eccentricities which issued from the Transcendental ferment. Ever more dissatisfied with civilization, he abruptly headed west in 1854, settled in an abandoned cabin in Warren County, Missouri, and supporting himself by hunting and fishing, lived the life of a hermit, pondering questions regarding "whence we come and whither we go."[1]

Just ripe for New England Transcendentalism, he had plunged headforemost into that oceanic swell and, with genuine hunger of the soul, appropriated the whole of it, carrying the transcendental notions of freedom, individualism, originality, and worship of nature to their extreme conclusions. His flight from the established social order to the backwoods of Missouri was nothing plaintive like Emerson's bidding goodbye to a "proud world." The Yankee experiments in living, at Brook Farm, Fruitlands, and elsewhere, were diminutive compared with the way of life he adopted for himself and the colonization scheme which he effected in Illinois about 1856. Thoreau's famed flight to his shanty on Walden Pond was an inconsequential lark compared with Brokmeyer's life in the primeval forest of Warren County, Missouri. Denton Jacques Snider, who had unusual opportunities for observing both the Eastern Transcendentalists and the Western Hegelians, though he considered the latter to have derived from the former, remarked that Brokmeyer was the only one of those who, receiving their primary impact from the Transcendental movement of New England, carried out its theories to their logical conclusions. He transcended Transcendentalism—both literally or practically and ideally or philosophically. His transcendence was two-fold: first, he lived the life strictly according to the vision which most of the theorists among his New England brethren contented themselves with advising others to follow, and second, he soon outgrew their ideas and superimposed upon their prevailingly Kantian romanticism a Hegelian superstructure of speculative thought.

The loss of his small fortune through the failure of an investment house was compensated by his discovery of Hegel about this time. In Hegel he seems to have found answers to his questions sufficient at least partially to reconcile himself to the ways of the world, for in 1856 he adopted St. Louis as his future home and moved thither his guns, fishing tackle, and chest of books, containing Thucydides, Homer, Sophocles, Aristophanes, Plato, Aristotle, Goethe, Hegel, Shakespeare, Moliere, Calderon, Cervantes, and Sterne. Forsaking his former trades, he turned ironmolder, prospered by his industry and ingenuity, indulged in land speculations, and became active on many fronts, meanwhile zealously consecrating his evenings to his precious books and permitting no interruptions except to frequent the haunts of small groups devoted to political and philosophical discussion.

At one of these informal meetings in 1858 Brokmeyer met Harris, the second in the triumvirate that was soon to be formed. The latter had come to St. Louis the year before, after a peripatetic education in New England terminated by two and a half years at Yale, where, during his junior year, a warning voice in chapel against the "new philosophical infidelity" of Alcott had made him a regular attendant at the Orphic Seer's Conversations early in 1857. He now threw aside all his "phrenological theories, mesmerism, spiritualism, the water-cure, vegetarianism, socialism, and all manner of reforms," and rating the two weeks during which he sat at the feet of Alcott his period of salvation, resigned from Yale and prepared for his *Wanderjahre*. A few months later he turned up in St. Louis as a teacher of the then novel Pitman shorthand, found employment in the St. Louis public schools, and rose, in a decade, to become Superintendent of the entire system. In 1865, when he visited Alcott in Concord, Mrs. Alcott commented upon the extraordinary resemblance between Harris and her husband as she recalled him at the time of their first meeting.[2]

Thus endowed and prepared, Harris found Brokmeyer a fascinating man. Voluble, bewhiskered, wiry of build, agile of movement, eyes alert ("the quick, almost wild eye of the hunter"), Brokmeyer presented a striking figure as he stood up, not at all chagrined by his workingman's clothes, to defend his position against all comers. His most prominent feature was "an enormous nose, somewhat crooked, which had the power of flattening and bulging and curveting and crooking in a variety of ways expressive of what was going on within him."[3] Eyes flashing and hands flailing the air, he boomed forth wisdom, wit, and profanity; then quite suddenly he would settle back at ease in a chair, cock high his heels, and with half-shut eyes ponder some profundity as he puffed at his "perpetual and vicious pipe."[4]

They were immediately fast friends, Harris becoming the pupil and Brokmeyer his tutor in Hegel. Together they conspired to spiritualize a frontier society by Hegelizing it. It was decided that the future salvation of the nation lay in translating Hegel's *Logic,* for only Hegel could save the nation from itself. Harris and two kindred "respectable vagabonds" pooled their slender resources to pension Brokmeyer to the extent of food and lodging while he made a literal translation of the monumental *Logic*—the first draft of which he completed during 1859-1860, when the war broke out, and Brokmeyer "swapped off" his Hegel for Hardie's *Infantry Tactics.* A few weeks later he found himself a colonel in the Union Army. Harris remained in St. Louis to keep the home fires burning.[5]

The war over, Brokmeyer, now a hero, returned, set up a law office, entered politics, was elected to the State Senate, wrote the state constitution of 1875, was elected Lieutenant Governor, and served as Governor during 1876-1877, when Governor Phelps was ill.

Harris, meanwhile, had kept a small group together and had gathered recruits, chief of whom was Snider, who had come to St. Louis, shortly after Appomattox, to teach in the Christian Brothers College. The Philosophical Society which came into existence in 1866 was the result less of a formal effort at organization than a finding-one-another-out and a coming-together of like-minded spirits. Having just gone through the cataclysm of war and finding themselves in the throes of reconstruction, in a fluid, volatile frontier society, they were fully prepared to listen to Brokmeyer, who combined speculative power with vigorous action, and who counselled that the only way out of a rampant materialism, invidious agnosticism, and despairing pessimism was to follow the "everlasting verities, the eternal principles, the pure Essences" of Hegelian absolutism.[6]

He argued well. He showed them the Hegelian solution of the dilemma with which the times confronted them. Hegel's doctrine that for a man to understand anything, he must see it in its relations, held for them a large meaning: all that is finite is provisional, no antagonisms are final, and all objects and all institutions are but phases of a process referable to a dialectic of thesis, antithesis, and synthesis.

These Hegelian principles and their implications struck the bewildered group of young intellectuals groping about in a chaos of disunion, war, and reconstruction in a "border" state with compelling force, and they adopted them *in toto* as a rationale. The leaders, ambitious to get the whole lesson, sought to master the intricacies of Hegel's abstruse dialectic, and some of them doubtless succeeded markedly. The lesser lights, satisfied with being practical idealists, contented themselves with Brokmeyer's and Harris' explanations. Hegel's involved logic and his dialectical subtleties they regarded as merely the professional philosopher's jargon for those principles which every practical man knows and applies without triadic mental gymnastics. Hegelian thought, notably in its practical applications and implications, fitted the men and the time of St. Louis.

There are several factors that suggest how but do not explain why the St. Louis Movement occurred in St. Louis instead of in one or several of a half-dozen other cities in the Mississippi Valley. They hint no reason why Harris, for example, quit Yale and turned up to teach shorthand in St. Louis rather than in Chicago or Milwaukee; why Brokmeyer walked out of the woods into St. Louis rather than Cincinnati or Detroit or elsewhere; nor why Snider, graduate of Oberlin, should engage himself by letter to teach in a Catholic college of St. Louis—all at about the same time. It has been said that the best explanation is the suggestion that winds of doctrine from Germany and similar winds from New England crossed each other's path in St. Louis and caused a rotary motion which whirled a goodly portion of the population up into the empyrean.[7]

But there are a number of causes that helped create the St. Louis Movement. One was the influx of New England Transcendentalism, whose proponents the several St. Louisans never wearied of apostrophizing as their masters, even while they sought to transcend them and their program.[8]

There was, in the next place, a strong contingent of Germans in St. Louis—many of them exiled intellectual idealists of 1848, trained in the German universities. They and their less cultivated countrymen fought side by side with their Anglo-American brethren to preserve the Union; upon their return they demanded and got their share of the spoils. The Germans of St. Louis made up Blair's hastily drummed-up little army that surprised and took Camp Jackson. This was the first decisive fight for the Federal Union: universal history pivoted momentarily on Camp Jackson. This daring act was interpreted as "The First Great St. Louis Deed."[9] Both Grant and Sherman were in St. Louis at the time as spectators, not participants. A month later both had cast off indecision and were colonels in the Union Army.

In the thick of the fight all the way, these Germans returned victorious, confident, and assertive. By 1864, the city council read like the roll of the Reichtag. The German language was introduced into the public schools, and bilingual citizenship was stoutly advocated. The Germans were in possession of the "city's control, material and spiritual."[10] The Teutonic influence spread. The constitutional convention of 1864-1865 chose a German for its president, and that of 1875 was completely dominated by Brokmeyer and his German supporters, including Joseph Pulitzer, who had risen to prominence by Brokmeyer's assistance, and who was by now editor and owner of the *Post-Dispatch*. When Finkelnburg was sent to Congress and Schurz to the United States Senate, the victory was complete. The capture of Washington and the transfer of the nation's capital to St. Louis seemed imminent!

"This upburst of domination of Germanism," says Snider, "I followed not from the outside but from the inside; I not only studied it as an object, but felt it and appropriated it till it became part of myself. And there were many natives here like me—many who experienced it as the uplift of a new strange spirit . . . as the revelation of the peculiar racial consciousness of old Teutonia welling forth just now on the banks of the Mississippi."[11] St. Louis was Teutonizing, and the Hegelian sense of Teutonic destiny ran subtly but powerfully through the entire population.

Predominantly Germanic though the movement was, both in its principles and in a considerable portion of its membership, all persons of Germanic origin were not therefore welcomed by the St. Louis philosophers. The several radical groups in the city, socialistic and communistic, were excluded; so were the immigrant laborer, the untutored, the boorish. Not that the working man was excluded because he worked; quite the contrary: he was as welcome as any other, but he had to demonstrate his eligibility to participate in the life of pure thought. Even Snider was required to pass muster by demonstrating his ability to translate a portion of Hegel's *Philosophy of Nature* before he was admitted to membership in the Philosophical Society. Proselyting was not carried on in the saloons, on the river front, or in the factories. Brokmeyer, "high-throned, Olympian," would tell you his message if asked "when in the right mood; but to go forth preaching it in the streets, not he!"[12] All conversations were held in Old Philosophers' Row—itself humble enough so far as worldly effects and exteriors indicated; but within burned the pure light of the Absolute. The members demanded of their fellows what Shelley asked of his mate: to feel poetry and understand philosophy.

Whatever foreign aspects the more popular phases

of the St. Louis Movement bore, the members of the Philosophical Society kept their eyes steadily on America—none more intently than Brokmeyer, the only foreign-born man among the leaders of the movement.[13] All the members sought to deepen their own thinking through the German philosophy which Brokmeyer proclaimed; but they cared little for Germany as such. It was America that they kept constantly in mind. So, too, their President. In leaving Germany in his youth, he had forsaken it for all time. He wasted no time romanticizing a lost Fatherland or indulging in escapist's fancies. His thought was for the United States of America, and his best-loved disciples were American-born. In these respects the St. Louis Movement is to be sharply distinguished from many another that began, continued, and ended as a Germanic *tour de force,* restricted to a purely German point of view and consequently destined to exert little influence beyond the sphere of its peculiarly isolated cultural "island" composed mainly of Germans and of German-Americans. The St. Louis Movement was thoroughly American in everything but inspiration.

Another powerful influence was a peculiar dualistic antagonism between theory and practice, of which the disciples of Hegel themselves were not at the time fully aware. On the one hand, they were devoted, heart and mind, to the life of absolutely pure and free thought; on the other, they had enthusiasm for and uncritical faith in the Great Illusion of the time that St. Louis was the Future Great City of the World. A remarkable energy, a unique cultural outburst, unbounded aspiration of individuals, along with grandiose civic ambition were felt throbbing upwards throughout the community. Snider felt it at once as the electrifying "city-soul, an all-dominating psychical trait . . . which [he says] I soon caught and then it caught me."[14]

After the census of 1880 had shattered the Grand Illusion and demonstrated that the "wicked Sodom" to the north of them had withstood even the wrath of God that had been visited upon Chicago in the form of the Great Fire, and that Chicago had actually outstripped the "world's coming Metropolis" in the race for size, wealth, power, and splendor,—even then many clung to their illusion and declared the United States Bureau of the Census to be in league with the forces of evil to subvert the good and the beautiful. The best mathematician of Washington University was engaged to check the names and the arithmetic of the census tabulation and to give the official census-taker the lie. Faith in the approaching triumph of the Great Continental Capital had been so long axiomatic in every mouth and on every street corner that it took some time for the bare, cold fact of Chicago's supremacy to dispel the illusion. By 1885

the Grand Illusion had made way for the Great Disillusion. Meanwhile the twenty years lying between
1865 and 1885 had sufficed to combine a pregnant
idea with a powerful *Zeitgeist* and to revive the most
energetic and pervasive idealistic movement that the
United States of America had felt since their formation into a nation.

Finally, it should be observed concerning the movement that its leaders took to heart their mentor's ad-
vice to practice self-activity, to realize themselves, to
translate thought into action.[15] They turned to literature, the arts, education and psychology, politics and
politically theory, law, religion, economics, social institutions, actively prosecuting reforms in all of them
and publishing books in all these fields. While the
St. Louis Movement produced a veritable avalanche
of books,[16] its members failed to bring forth a single
book which can be called a literary success. New
England Transcendentalism owed much of its success, propagation, and permanence of influence to
the excellence of its literature; the St. Louis Movement failed to get into print even the book from
which it professed to draw its inspiration and susten-
ance, Brokmeyer's competent but overliteral translation of Hegel's *Logic*.

The vicissitudes of this manuscript, of which
numerous copies circulated among the several
groups of idealists, are too intricate to relate in

full. One copy served the Hegelian Club, under the guidance of Samuel Emery, at Quincy, Illinois; another was read by the Plato Club, founded by Dr. Hiram K. Jones, at Jacksonville, Illinois; Harris carried a third with him to Concord and, after he became U. S. Commissioner of Education, to Washington, D. C.; fragments have recently turned up in New Hampshire; and a part of the last draft which Brokmeyer thumbed through during his last days is deposited in the library of the Missouri Historical Society.

While the successive publishers who refused to print Brokmeyer's translation demonstrated their sagacity as business men, the historians of American philosophy who have dismissed Brokmeyer's version as incomprehensible apparently did not take the trouble to examine it. Its only fault is that it is so literally true to the original of Hegel that the reader who is unfamiliar with the involved Teutonic sentence structure finds the reading extremely wearisome. But it is clear that Brokmeyer knew his Hegel, and there is every indication that he interpreted the Hegelian logic correctly to his students. Yet the "great Bible of the Movement remained, in the end, in the voluble and expansive genius of Brokmeyer," whence neither his own heroic efforts nor the combined and almost cabalistic efforts of his friends succeeded in extracting a printable draft.

Lest an erroneous conclusion be drawn from these representations, it should be added that the twenty-two volumes of the *Journal of Speculative Philosophy* (1867-1888), the first periodical in the English-speaking world devoted exclusively to speculative philosophy, provide formidable evidence that the members of the St. Louis School possessed something more than ebulition. Yet, in the final analysis, it is true that they were all super-individualists who took so literally their master's precept to realize their individual potentialities that they were incapable of carrying through any truly cooperative practical undertaking. So long as Brokmeyer—"a thinker," in Harris' estimation, "of the same order of mind as Hegel"[17]—remained among them, he was both Hegel and Hegel's *Logic*. So long as his philosophical genius, "equal to that of Hegel and more poetical" (says Snider)[18] stood by, they needed no Canonical Book. Time and again Brokmeyer would, by "one lightning flash of his consuming logic," resolve their doubts and explain their queries. He was "the primal Titanic demiurge"[19] of the Movement, he held them together, giving them a kind of unity, however much Kroeger, the Fichtean among them, chafed at the bit, and Davidson, the Aristotelean and jolly free-lance, kicked over the traces. But when Brokmeyer left without giving them the great Bible to chart the way, the several individuals asserted their individualism, each bent on "self-activity." That commandment of their master's they had learned complete. A Brook Farm Association or any other collaborative or communistic enterprise would have been beyond the realm of possibility for them. Indeed, Brokmeyer himself set the example for "self-determination." Like Thoreau's, the primary passion of his life was to be utterly himself, to go his own way, apart from the crowd. An idealistic exile, journeyman, steel-worker, huntsman, soldier, lawyer, and philosopher, he next turned statesman and finally hermit. Disillusioned in his hopes of making Hegelianism prevail, and disappointed in politics, when a returned Southerner defeated him in a senatorial contest, he turned his back once more upon civilization and found employment that permitted him to indulge his love for the elemental and the natural. His sorties into the farther West became more frequent and prolonged. For some years he lived among the Creek Indians of the Oklahoma Territory, where he sought to persuade Snider to join him and start a kindergarten among the Indian children of Muskegee, while he himself would explain the deeper philosophy of deer-stalking to the warriors in terms of Hegelian dialectics. The Indians conferred upon him the title of "Great White Father" and offered him his choice of the fairest maidens of the tribe—an offer which his Hegelianism compelled him regretfully to decline.

From 1880 to 1896 he vacillated between the wilderness and civilization, appearing occasionally to contribute a lecture to the numerous schools which his friends arranged in Milwaukee, St. Louis, Cincinnati, and elsewhere, or revising his translation of Hegel's *Logic*, meanwhile shipping numerous mahogany and rosewood saplings back to St. Louis, where, at his leisure, he whittled out beautifully polished walking sticks for his friends, frugally utilizing the chips for equally aesthetic toothpicks, carefully cut in three sizes and bottled with elaborately carved stoppers. The remaining ten years of his life were spent in St. Louis in quiet pursuits, chief of which was his re-translation of the *Logic*. He died on July 26, 1906, in his seventy-eighth year. Asked on his deathbed what disposition was to be made of his manuscript, he replied: "Just leave it in the attic for the vermin; I have enjoyed every minute of my life devoted to it, in the hope that I might justify my existence by leaving something to posterity worthwhile, but apparently there is no demand for anything like that at this time."[20]

Such was the melancholy end of the man who, while he was among the associated philosophers of St. Louis, put an interpretation upon current events and living issues that enabled them to read a significance of meaning into the contemporary scene that was perhaps more portentous than the cold facts of history have as yet made clear. But back in the seventies, given (1) the dramatic episodes of the struggle for national unity, (2) a strong German contingent in St. Louis dedicated to humanitarianism and social and political reform, and (3) a boundless West to which St. Louis was the gateway, it was inevitable that St. Louisans should seize upon the romantic features of Hegelian thought by which to bring order out of chaos and to give interpretation and purpose to the rôle that St. Louis was to play in a frontier society. Hegel was the philosopher of progress, or advance. He was also the proponent of absolute, pure thought. Above all, he was the reconciler of opposites. The young men of St. Louis eagerly seized upon him as pointing the way to reconciling materialism and idealism, individual statehood and federal unionism, rights and duties, faith and knowledge, spiritualism and naturalism. Viewed in the light of American civilization as a whole, the St. Louis Movement is a phase of the conflict between the naturalism and supernaturalism that characterized the nineteenth century generally, a phase of that long crisis, partly religious, when many a clear-headed thinker of the time saw but one alternative: to avow himself either a medieval man and a Christian or a modern man and a skeptic.[21]

This conflict which the St. Louisans inherited and sought to arbitrate is, in a sense, the cumulative result of many years of controversy. The path of its development, even in its purely native beginnings, is hard to retrace, but surely William Ellery Channing's sermon at the ordination of Jared Sparks in Baltimore (1819) is one of the milestones, and Emerson's *Divinity School Address* (1838), the Norton-Ripley controversy (1839-1840), and Theodore Parker's South Boston sermon on *The Transient and Permanent in Christianity* (1841) are others. When the St. Louis Movement began, the difference between what Parker called the transient and the permanent in religion had not been so sharply drawn nor were they so clearly understood as they are today. The drawing of this distinction between religion itself on the one hand and the expression of religion in doctrines and rites, or the application of religion through institutions, on the other, is one of the great achievements of the nineteenth century. Thanks to the St. Louis philosophers and to the influence of many scholars in other circles and associations, the twentieth century no longer has the same difficulty in distinguishing between the transient and the permanent in historic religion; no longer so easily confuses the real with its accidents, the kernel with the husk.

The men of St. Louis were distinguished more for

their aloofness from churches than for their adherence to religious creeds. Emerson, when he first met the group, half jocularly but approvingly spoke of Harris and his "German Atheists." [22] They neither were nor became apostles of any form of religious dogma or theological doctrine; but they were, to a man, profoundly religious and thoughtful—intent upon nothing less than the solution of the fundamental problems of man. They were philosophers of the kind whose philosophy impinges at every point on religion. They professed themselves to be, and were, disciples of the Kantian Reason and the Hegelian Logic; but they stopped short of applying only the understanding or the pure reason to their problems. Harris printed as a motto for the *Journal of Speculative Philosophy* a passage from Novalis: "Philosophy can bake no bread, but she can procure for us God, Freedom, and Immortality." What he meant by this was something very practical—in no way either esoteric or precisely scientific. With certain tendencies of twentieth-century philosophic inquiry they would have had little sympathy, as for instance, with the aspiration to be strictly scientific in the sense in which physics and geology are scientific. The pure essences which they sought, they were convinced, were not discoverable by any *one* of man's mental powers or by any such procedure as the scientific agnostic employs. Truth, Beauty, and Goodness were not to be analyzed by chemical techniques or measured in physical terms. Nor were they mystics, content with soul-satisfying but fundamentally irrational intuitions. Harris explained, in the first number of the *Journal of Speculative Philosophy,* that he and his associates would not accept tradition unmodified; neither would they break with it altogether. They were men who had been nourished on Christian conceptions; they sought a philosophy which would enable them, without sacrificing their intellectual integrity, to reconcile the measurable facts of science with the immeasurable concepts of the heart and soul.[23]

Materialism and naturalism had received a strong impetus from the uniformitarian geology of Sir Charles Lyell. The significance of the new science had struck thinking men so forcibly that many sincere theologians as well as pious scientists set zealously to work to harmonize geology with Genesis. Just as the Christian apologists of eighteenth-century England found themselves ultimately playing into the hands of the natural religionists and scientific deists, so now the orthodox began to suspect that whether they used the traditional weapons of defense or employed those of the enemy, the scientific attack would prove invincible. Then followed in rapid succession Darwin's *Origin of Species,* Huxley's explanations of the evolutionary philosophy, and Spencer's

First Principles, which, in spite of their unknowable quantities, are still essentially naturalistic. Allied as young idealists like Harris and Snider felt these foreign importations to be with the already rampant American materialism, the rising tide of naturalism, supported by the apparently irresistible might of science, seemed to bear down all opposition and to leave nothing save meaningless evolutions of matter determined by mindless mechanism. The Synthetic Philosophy of Herbert Spencer, together with the causes that lay before him, the allies that joined him, and the effects that succeeded him, the St. Louisans singled out to attack and overcome. Harris, whose career is most readily followed, and whose philosophical course is most consistently straightforward, set his face against the Atomists, the Sophists, the Brahmanists, the Eleatics, against Spinoza, Hamilton, Hume, Rousseau, Mill, Comte, Cousin, Spencer, and all others whose teachings led, in his opinion, to mechanism, materialism, pantheism, agnosticism, or atheism. To put it another way, we may say that Harris, in conformity with the Hegelian precept and example, fought less against any one or all of these than against the presumption of any one of them to be the only true system. "After all," wrote Harris, in the preface to the first volume of the *Journal,* "it is not American *thought* so much as American *thinkers* that we want." He saw as clearly as does the man of the twentieth century that mechanism is an excellent, even indispensable, hypothesis in scientific research, but miserably inadequate as a philosophy. Conversely, he attentively studied the various oriental mysticisms for what they hold that might be of value in making the final synthesis, but he consistently denied that they, either individually or collectively, represented the whole truth. For him, one was thesis; the other, antithesis; what was wanted was the proper synthesis, a "correlation of forces," a reconciliation of two opposites, neither one of which alone was wholly true or wholly false but merely, in and of itself, inadequate. In short, he sought in the speculative the point at which "the two are one."

But we should be very wide the mark if we assumed that the motivating force behind the movement was theological or philosophical, *i.e.* merely theoretical. Its center of gravity at the beginning was political and practical. A political refugee, thoroughly schooled in the life of random experience, Brokmeyer was inspired by Hegelianism as a gospel of social and political salvation. In the urgent social milieu of the border state Missouri in which he found himself "the flint of Brokmeyer struck fire."[24] He could hardly have hit upon a solvent theory better suited to bring order out of chaos or upon a more systematic defense of his faith than Hegel's. He knew both Hegel's speculative and practical philosophy. Both, he assumed, would be equally practicable; but the present crisis cried for practical action. His enthusiasm for the Hegelian theory of social progress and the construction of a humanitarian Utopia was thoroughly aroused. When the meetings in Old Philosophers' Row were held, three of the group— Brokmeyer, and the two Judges, Horatio M. Jones and Johann G. Woerner—were already actively engaged in politics. Together they considered and discussed the dialectic of politics and political parties and impending problems, which necessarily involved the fundamental nature of the state. Of most basic concern was the relation of the Federal government to the single states which composed it, and the means to prevent each from devouring the other. The uncontrolled desire of both to do precisely that during the decade just past had resulted in the debacle, from the consequences of which the men of their generation were trying to extricate themselves. They studied political theorists; they delved into the Constitution of the United States; they planned a philosophical book upon the subject (which never materialized unless we accept Judge Woerner's *Rebel's Daughter,* a novel with an elaborate presentation of political points of view and arguments); but especially did they pore over Hegel's philosophy of the state and discuss its strengths and weaknesses and its applicability to the United States in the sixties.[25]

To them nothing seemed clearer than that Hegel was the prophet of a reunited nation after it had suffered the terrible "dialectic" of civil war. Brokmeyer, then playing the most prominent rôle among them as lawyer and statesman, assumed the position of tutor to explain that the Southern position was what Hegel termed that of "abstract right"; the Northern, that of an equally "abstract morality"; and the United States, that which was synonymous with Hegel's "ethical State." This idea is clearly stated by Harris in his prefatory remarks "To the Reader" in number one of the *Journal*. At once faithful to the Hegelian principle that the history of the world is the progress of liberty, and obedient to the letter, as well as to the spirit, of the master, they did not shrink from the conflict, but met it, confident that no real synthesis in history is possible except through "the tragic process of the dialectic of events."[26]

These circumstances explain the rumble of the Hegelian triadic movement that runs through the written record of these Hegel-intoxicated men and women. Held together by the zealous Brokmeyer, they vied with each other in applying the fixed formula of Hegel to every phase of the gigantic struggle. Thus, Fort Sumter was the "thesis," Camp Jackson the "antithesis," and the declaration of war the "synthesis." Again, the great real estate boom, or "illusion" in St. Louis was the "thesis," the founding of the Philosophical Society the "antithesis," and the building of the great Eads Bridge the "synthesis." The Hegelian dogma was applied even to the rivalry between St. Louis and Chicago. The rise of the latter was in "antithesis" to St. Louis. Unshamefacedly they hailed the great fire as the conclusion of the "phase," following which St. Louis would be free to establish the hoped-for "synthesis." In 1890, Harris recalled that they used the Hegelian dialectic to solve "all problems connected with school-teaching and school-management," and that "even the hunting of turkeys and squirrels was the occasion for the use of philosophy."[27] He emphasized the applicability and significance of the Hegelian dialectic again and again in the *Journal*. While Judge Johann Gabriel Woerner refrained from putting it as badly as did Harris and Snider in their less literary works, nevertheless, the idea of *The Rebel's Daughter, A Story of Love, Politics and War*, involving as it does the clash of Southern and Northern ideas, turns upon this same development of thought; and Miss Anna C. Brackett early enshrined the Hegelian triad in some verses entitled "Comprehension," ending:

. . . only where the one is twain,
And where the two are one again,
Will truth no more be sought in vain.

By circumstances and thought processes such as these was the West Hegelized and the stage prepared for the appearance of the benign Alcott and the burly Brokmeyer in the same arena. There followed some diverting antics, beneath the comical exterior of which, however, none who witnessed the fun failed to realize that two diametrically opposed systems of thought were involved, or to believe that according to the way this duel went, would go the course of American thought.

II. ALCOTT AMONG THE HEGELIANS

The creation of the Philosophical Society in St. Louis and the organization of the Hegelians of the West into a visible body set the stage upon which William Torrey Harris decided in 1866 to show off his friend from "back East." The membership of the Society would provide Amos Bronson Alcott of Concord, Massachusetts, with "fit audience though few." Thus it came to pass that the saintly Alcott found himself sharing the spotlight with Brokmeyer, the backwoods philosopher, during the second week of February, 1866. Nothing was further from Harris' design or Alcott's intention than that this stage should be turned into an arena for gladiatorial combat. But neither had yet sufficiently recognized the fact that the only thing about Brokmeyer that could be predicted with certainty was his unpredictability.

Alcott had, in fact, met Brokmeyer on his first trip to St. Louis, back in 1859, when Harris had invited him to "converse" with the first, pre-war group of philosophers, then meeting in lodging rooms of the members. His first visit to the St. Louisans had not turned out altogether and mutually satisfactorily to all concerned, mainly because they wanted to hear about his idealistic philosophy, and he wanted to tell them about communal experiments and underground railways. For his part, he was impressed by his first contact with systematic thinking, very different from the kind in which he and Emerson indulged; but he found his first acquaintance with it neither highly profitable nor wholly pleasant, so that when he returned home late in February, he was glad to be back among men who thought in grooves more familiar to him. The touch of Hegelianism to which he had been subjected was soon obscured by his return to the Bible, Plato, Aristotle, and Swedenborg, his election to the superintendency of the Concord Public Schools, and the John Brown affair. As a metaphysician, Alcott was just the same in 1866, when he revisited St. Louis, as he had been seven years earlier.[28]

On the former occasion Brokmeyer had kept the peace, for in 1859 he was not yet the high and mighty commander of men. Although he was already unquestionably the best Hegelian among them and a master dialectician, he had not yet won fame in the Civil War, the Philosophical Society had not yet been formed, and he was not yet the duly elected President. So he contented himself with cursing his friend William Hyde of the *Missouri Republican,* who had persuaded him to give up for an evening his beloved books to hear this wise man of the East, as Harris persisted in calling him, but who, on nearer examination, had turned out to be an unmitigated charlatan parading about in the nineteenth century in the cast-off rags and tags of second and third-rate Neo-Platonists. For the rest of his steam, he let it off harmlessly in his diary, by calling Alcott mild names, such as "peddler" of "infantile assininities" of "mummy wrappage," the result of having "burrowed round until he hit upon the works of Iamblichus and Plotinus," whom he had not had the honesty to read or the power to comprehend. "If he had penetrated to their thought, he would not be peddling emanation theories with Pythagorean dietary notions, and cut up shines, such as are reported of him, as a member of society and a citizen of the State."[29]

If Alcott had known the animosity he aroused in

Brokmeyer, he might not have been as eager as he was to accept Harris' urgent invitation to address the newly formed Philosophical Society. Indeed, it seems that Harris had, in a measure, mismanaged the affair; certainly he had not shown his usual circumspection. The Society had been formed on January 22, ostensibly to gather support for the publication of Brokmeyer's translation of Hegel's *Logic*. President Brokmeyer had been asked to institute the programs of the Society by presenting his exegesis of *Faust*, a work which he ranked as high in poetry as he rated Hegel's *Logic* in philosophy, and which always provoked his greatest eloquence. Then it developed that apparently Harris had hurried up the organization of the Society itself primarily to have it in readiness to receive Alcott and to provide him with a select group of auditors. Brokmeyer had delivered only the first of his discourses on *Faust* when Alcott appeared on February 9, 1866. Brokmeyer did not like the looks of things.

Alcott was accorded a "hearty reception" by Harris at his home in "Salisbury Street between Ninth and Tenth Streets." That afternoon Harris took him to "an informal meeting of the Philosophical Society in Mr. Hill's rooms," where Alcott met Brokmeyer, Dr. Watters of the St. Louis Medical School, Dr. Hall, Mr. Hill, an attorney, Judge J. G. Woerner, very probably Snider, and others.[30] Though they talked about Hegel, Fichte, and Eastern and Western life and thought, they also talked about *Faust*. Brokmeyer was not to be denied his say about *Faust* even though the distinguished guest had come all the way from Concord to converse with them about his theory of "Lapse." For his part, Alcott immediately put down Brokmeyer as "a man of original genius." Unsuspectingly he added, "His thoughts on *Faust* are surprisingly fresh and new; also on the prairie life as influencing the common sense of the resident."[32] Those who knew their fiery president knew what Brokmeyer was driving at: he was spoiling for a fight. Alcott did not know it—not yet!

Meanwhile Alcott went on to confide to his journal, blithely and glowingly, "My friends have arranged for my meeting them at Mr. Hill's room on Tuesday and Thursday evenings for discussing philosophy, and have a popular course on Wednesday and Friday evenings at private houses, as the company find convenient. Plainly they propose to hold me busy while I am with them, both in public and private interviews. My wish is to compare views generally with them—philosophical, literary, social—and meet, in such ways as open naturally, any who may care to see me."[33] In this expansive mood he again broached the subject already mentioned during his first visit seven years earlier, namely, that Harris should undertake "a biographical account of him when he should complete his earthly career," and he went on to dictate to Harris "an inventory of his spiritual real estate."[34]

The same night several of the Society met again at Harris' house "for comparing thoughts a little— Brokmeyer, Watters, Hall, Hill, Martling, Kroeger." Here Alcott had his opportunity to unfold his "hierarchy of lives theory . . . the descent of souls from pure being, the Person, through mind; thence by lapsed minds generating matter, as seen in the scale of organized bodies; from idea to atom— nature being the surplussage of mind, and man the relic." This provoked "much questioning all around, and attempted reconciliation of theories." "They tell me," Alcott added, "I am an Hegelian in spirit if not in form, and seem disposed to claim me as of their master's school. I am more desirous of seeing than saying, and think far better of the gift of divining than of reasoning—of the seer's sight than of philosophizing."[35]

At the suggestion that Alcott was a Hegelian, Brokmeyer sniffed audibly. But he kept the peace, except to make quite clear (1) that he had trouble following Alcott's theory of "Lapse," or emanation, by which Alcott could derive, through some process of reasoning incomprehensible to Brokmeyer, from the indestructible, unsayable One any resultant at all, thus making a reduction from an irreducible and unknown God-head to a known atom, and (2) that he cared not a fig for divining as against reasoning.[36] Thus the flame was kindled and nourished; for a week longer Brokmeyer listened and restrained the demon seething within him. Meanwhile Alcott continued on his rounds, all planned for him by Harris.

On his second day in St. Louis Alcott called, with Harris, on Dr. Watters and Dr. Hall, spoke before two hundred of the assembled St. Louis Association of Teachers on the subject of "the ideal teacher," dined with Dr. Watters, and passed the evening with Harris, who surprised him with his energy, enthusiasm, and great aims: "[He] thinks of translating— aided by his friends here—most of Hegel's works. Has already completed the Logic, Aesthetics, parts of the History of Philosophy, Philosophy of Nature; and will simply write an introduction to the study and genius of Hegel."[37] This Western resourcefulness and activity made Alcott's head swim.

Two days later, after further conversations, he observed that "Harris, Brokmeyer, Kroeger, Watters, Howison, Tafel—all men of good ambitions and given to earnest thinking"—would bear watching. "I am to find," he mused, "whether theirs is not the task the East has failed to complete, whether these men may not carry forward and complement the thought of New England."[38] It would be interesting to know whether this thought occurred to him of his own accord, or whether Harris planted it in Alcott's mind; for Harris was as anxious to unite the West with the East as Brokmeyer, Snider, and others of the Westerners were to maintain their own status.

If, on the sixteenth, at Brokmeyer's room, Alcott said anything about Brokmeyer's fledglings "complementing" his own and Emerson's thought, Brokmeyer may well have dropped some hints that led Alcott to observe a bit tartly in his journal that night that he "cared less for" Brokmeyer's discourse on "his part in the Missouri troubles, and talk about politics, his colonelcy, representing his county in the St. Louis legislature, etc. . . . than for his criticism of Goethe and philosophy."[39] That evening, "hoarse" as he was, he conversed to "a good company gathered at Kroeger's house" on the subject of "home," and found that here in the West, "as in Eastern circles, religion steals into any high discussion . . . and the sectarians persist on having all told that one may have thought in his heart." To Alcott, who liked to observe some of his New England reticences, no less than did Emerson, this outspoken frankness among these Westerners was a bit disconcerting. But Kroeger as host "knew how to manage his neighbors, and, though Howison spoke like the schoolman he is, and Harris like a dialectician, the Puritan per-

sisted, and drew out his questions interminable."
Nevertheless, he considered the evening a success:
"The clear sailing came at last . . . and the evening
was voted suggestive and wholesome."[40] Brokmeyer
had been absent, while Snider, still feeling himself
a philosopher novice, had not ventured to speak out
of turn.

At the next session the storm broke. Snider had
been restive from the first under the bombardment
of Alcott's "mystic oracles—often dark, tortuous,
and riddlesome." As the meeting progressed, Alcott's
manner of reading in a "sepulchral tone" from slips
of paper and his habit of throwing down the slips
as if to say, "There, gentlemen, what say you to
that?" got on Snider's nerves.[41] On this particular
evening some twenty men had gathered "into a kind
of circle before the new Orpheus;" directly in front
of the prophet sat Brokmeyer, eyes alert and mis-
chievous, ready to act both as chief interpreter and
hierophant. But Alcott soon began to suspect that
as a mouthpiece Brokmeyer was not altogether trust-
worthy. Brokmeyer's performance that night puzzled
everybody, even Snider. To some of Alcott's oracles
Brokmeyer "would give an easy sober significance,
which we all understood, but others he seemed to
turn inside out and then to shiver into smithereens."
Finally he picked up one which had just been read,
and "at the fiery touch of his dialectics, set off with

his Mephistophelean chuckle, he simply exploded it into mist with a sort of detonation, as if it were a soap bubble filled with explosive gas."[42] At this point Alcott began to realize that, by some Hegelian process which he did not understand, his oracles were being made to contradict themselves and himself. He grew testy, as a man well might; then he lost his temper; and finally, raising his voice, said in a loud, raucous tone such as one would hardly have suspected him capable of, "Mr. Brokmeyer, you confound us with the multiplicity of your words and the profusion of your fancy." "This," says Snider, "was the first wholly intelligible saying of Orpheus that evening, and certainly the most impressive." Brokmeyer, visibly restraining himself and recollecting that he was Mr. Alcott's host, replied calmly, "Perhaps I do;" but it was evident to the men trained in Hegelian logic at "Brokmeyer University" that if it ever came to a serious intellectual tussle between this "poor old man, thin in thews and in thought," and their Titanic President, the New Englander would leave "not a philosophic grease-spot."[43]

Harris, seeing that Brokmeyer was in one of his Rabelaisian humors, not merely teasing but provoking, tried to step into the breach and to smooth things over. The reading went on, "not in its pristine vigor," but it went on. Snider remembered distinctly that it went on until ten o'clock, the discussion zig-zagging about in all sorts of twists and turns above and below the surface. Then Alcott read: "It requires a Christ to interpret a Christ." Snider awoke. The remark aroused his risibilities. He asked himself: "Has this foxy Yankee just coined this little oracle on Brokmeyer, or on Harris, or on all of us together, with himself in the background?" At the thought of this possible treachery, he arose and delivered himself of his only remark of the evening:

"Gentlemen, [if] I may be permitted to state my interpretation of this last saying: its hidden meaning is, in my judgment, that only an Alcott can rightly interpret an Alcott. That being the case, we all had better now go home."

At this un-apostolic deliverance, little titters and tee-hees went round the circle, people reached for their hats, and Orpheus himself, looking at Snider somewhat oracularly, impatiently shut up his map of oracles and followed the others out.[44]

After such an experience Alcott came home and reflected, a bit sadly but very honestly: "If wanting in the courtesies of conversation, these western minds take every freedom of tart debate and drive home the argument at a fearful rate. Customs, traditions, which we call deference to authorities, they hold as embarrassing and set them rudely aside, ignore them altogether. 'Tis refreshing to see, and worth the journey. Nothing better for dissolving superstitions than beholding at first sight . . . I see not what chance of hearing a mere scholar and bigot has here in these free wild parts. And though I value the reserves more than most, loving the sacred names and persons as I find few of my contemporaries [do], this free, frolicsome, slovenly sense of able earnest men·has a formidable attraction, and carries the logic of an argument seldom reached by our well-behaved populations. One can spare the courtesy for this candor, and caution for the conviction—discretion being here the worser valor, and too slow in the race. After the thought will follow the manners, and this new New England will compete in all things with the land of its ancestry, the school of its culture."[45]

How Brokmeyer would have snorted if he could have read this judgment upon his manners and the implication that he and his confreres were only adjuncts of the idealistic movement bred in Concord! Nonetheless, whatever we may think of Alcott's philosophy, we must recognize the fact that the man had insight.

The truth of the matter is that there was from the beginning a good deal of mistrust on the part of some of the St. Louis Hegelians of the Platonic Transcendentalists from the East. Snider, for example, had long wondered why Harris should insist on importing this "repeating sayer of the said to say again what had already been better said," and why he should be so assiduous in "admiring what he had often sufficiently admired."[46] When, toward the end of the seventies, Harris announced his intention of moving to Concord, Snider saw the light: Harris was going "to hitch the two horses, Concord and St. Louis, to his philosophical chariot."[47] An Easterner by birth and rearing, Harris could be forgiven his love for the rocks of New England; but Snider believed the effort "to capture and reconstruct" New England Transcendentalism a profound error. The true American philosophy, he felt, should be started anew and built from the ground up in the West, where it would have a chance to become truly expressive of America. He questioned Harris' wisdom in going to Concord at all, and foretold his failure.[48] His misgivings did not prevent his participating in five of the first seven summer sessions of the Concord School of Philosophy (1879-1887); but after the third, which he considered the most successful,[49] he felt that Westerners like himself, Harris, Emery, and Jones would be forever derided by the Concordians as "borderers," and he observed that some of the Easterners were none too enthusiastic about their own native sons.[50] Moreover, he soon felt Sanborn's "stinger" concealed in his "mellifluous" voice and "winsome smiles"; he suspected Emery's sincerity from the first. Hiram K. Jones' Platonism and W. T. Harris' Hegelianism seemed forever to provoke arguments which even the philosophic serenity of the presiding Alcott could not always assuage;[51] and when the disturbing subject of psychology, as promulgated by William James, reared its head, and Tom Davidson's learned sneer and paradoxical sardonicism confounded the confusion,[52] Snider, having already concluded that henceforth the course of the School would be downward, went fishing in Thoreau's Walden and interpreted his failure to get so much as a nibble as a sign that it was not destined for the St. Louisans to make any great haul of philosophical fishes in Concord.[53] "The Mississippi," he concluded, "could not be made to flow eastward through New England."[54] For himself, he said he had no genius for being "colonialized."[55] "My goal remained in the West; I had no Mayflower tradition to chain me to Plymouth Rock or to any other piece of stone."[56] Snider's life is a remarkable instance of the tenacity with which a man can cling to his life's purpose without deflection, in his case, to be "A Writer of Books."

Other meetings there were — many of them, for Emerson's "tedious archangel" remained "nearly four weeks," with "a distinct loss to his reputation," thought Snider, for "it became common to remark that he repeated himself and went backward after the first week."[57] But Harris, doubtless having the future Concord School already in view, sought to bolster him in every way. Snider grew thoroughly "tired" of Alcott and cared no longer to hear him "unless Brokmeyer were present to put pulsing vitality and huge substance into the rather thin Yankee gruel, always getting thinner."[58]

Still he remembered one notable evening when, it seems, Alcott went back to say in detail what he had, on his first day among them, said "loosely" on the hierarchy of lives, the descent of souls from pure being, "lapsed" minds generating matter, and the evolution of atom from idea—in short, "a full exposition of his doctrine of the lapse of soul, from the Primal One, dropping in its descent the various orders of creation down to matter." Brokmeyer was present, in his highest vein, but in a totally different mood from that which had possessed him during former prelections—everything Mephistophelean fallen away, ready to enter sympathetically into the "most earnest philosophical discussion of the deepest truth which can engage the human kind." When it came time for him to speak, he did so courteously and appreciatively, uttering "a pure stream of the brightest thought, his enthusiasm overflowing him like a torrent, overpowering him, carrying him away." But when he came to Alcott's "lapse of soul" theory, he did not pull his punches, pointing out that in this year 1866 it could not be considered anything more than a "relapse" to the old Neo-Platonic theory of emanation which had long been transcended.[59] What rage he felt at Alcott's parading the streets of St. Louis in the rags of Pythagoras, embellished, as he felt, with poor imitations of Neo-Platonic adornments, he vented on the pages of his diary, where it did the angelic Alcott no harm. Instead he calmly stressed the opposite movement—occidental evolution, Hegelian speculation, and the modern principle of freedom.

Once again Alcott found himself in the grip of a stronger philosophical mind than his own. He recalled an unhappy evening at Emerson's, back in the forties, when Emerson had invited to his home some people whom he wanted to make acquainted with the Orphic Sage—so that they might "know what a rare fellow he is." Among them had been Theodore Parker, of the "steel-cold intelligence," sharpened on German metaphysics. The evening had been a failure, for when Alcott's intuitions clashed with Parker's pure reason, Parker (says Emerson) "wound himself around Alcott like an anaconda; you could hear poor Alcott's bones crunch."[60] This more recent experience of coming squarely up against the systematic dialetical method of Brokmeyer gave Alcott food for thought. The "hard logical" grip of Brokmeyer, he concluded, was far more like an anaconda's than Parker's, when it came to "the crunching of transcendental bones."[61] On March 17, back in Concord, he found home "good and enjoyable . . . after these dreary days of travel and spent spirits." "Yet," he added, "I shall doubtless venture again into those wild parts"; and to reassure himself, he went over and had a talk with Emerson, then just returned from his "western tour where he has been lecturing for a month or more."[62] Three weeks later he was seriously reconsidering the claims of these Hegel-enraptured men of St. Louis: "It is claimed for Hegel that his dialectic is an organism of the spirit, like the mathematics of nature, completing for the mind what Plato and Aristotle attempted in their way. [The words are as if they were taken directly out of the mouths of Harris and Brokmeyer.] Certainly the uses to which Harris and Brokmeyer put it were surprising to me, and almost persuaded me that Hegel's claims are valid."[63] By July 20, he was reading Stirling's *Secret of Hegel*,[64] a gift to him from Louisa May; before the year was out, he had set forth again "to belt the continent with talk;"[65] and, as might be expected, he stopped in St. Louis to learn more and to take more punishment.

Thenceforth his journals contain many introspective passages in which he analyzed and searched himself for some assurance that he possessed a dialectic method and a systematic body of thought, generally concluding that he must rest content with his neighbor Emerson to divine rather than to rationalize.[66]

Nevertheless, he continued the quest. On July 18, 1871, following a discussion with Emerson and Harris of "the Hegelian thesis of Being," he concluded, "The Hegelian logic is strange and unintelligible to him [Emerson], as it is to myself; but I see what marvels it performs in the hands of a master like Harris, and owe it a deep respect."[67] Six months later he was forced to admit, however "humbling to New England pride," that while philosophical talk is cheap in Boston, "Philosophy is published in St. Louis,"[68] and by the end of 1872 he had coined a new word: "Westernize [he said] is a verb meaning *progress.*"[69] Those Westerners, their methods, and their accomplishments were not easy to disregard. Two years later he decided that "Method is everything . . . We moderns are deficient in method, and, so far, powerless. We need . . . the ancient dialectic, or the skill of accosting the mind by a knowledge of its laws of thought and volition. . . . The true logic, the ideal logic, walks abreast of the mind as a friend and prompter, a guide, not an agitator."[70]

In the end, when the Concord School had become a reality, and he had been named its head, Harris continued to pour into his ears fulsome flattery, and ultimately Alcott was brought to conclude happily, "I am not philosopher enough to know whether I am [a] philosopher in the strictest sense of pursuing a methodical habit of thinking. But if so competent a judge of method as Harris finds logic in it, calls it 'dialectic' or by any name known to philosophy, then I suppose I am entitled to the praise which he bestows on my thinking."[71] On occasions, however, he found it prudent to reassert his mysticism, as on the day when Harris and Jones waxed particularly warm. Alcott, striking a philosophic attitude, called them to order and, deprecating the apparent misunderstanding, suggested a "higher ground" upon which the two disputants might find a common footing, only to have both turn upon him with exclamations that they did not understand what he meant. As the worthy Dean subsided into his seat, he muttered, "Well, I don't know as I know what I mean myself," adding, as the audience tittered, "I am a mystic, you know."[72]

The Concord School became another arena for another clash between two defenders of the rival philosophies—the proponents this time being Dr. Jones the Platonist from Jacksonville and Dr. Harris the Hegelian from St. Louis. To Dean Alcott was reserved the happy function of moderator, his benign face shedding benevolence and his sepulchral voice commanding respect as he sought to restore peace and order when the debate grew warm and got out of hand. Brokmeyer was prevented from entering the fray by the simple expedient of not inviting him, lest he spill over into some irrepressible *diablerie,* as he had at Snider's Goethe Summer School in Mil waukee. In Concord it would not do to have him turn "a very unconventional somersault right in the presence of fastidious Lady Convention herself."[73] Anyway, he preferred Indians to Concordians. Meanwhile the first bout between East and West, between Alcott and Brokmeyer, between Plato and Hegel, was chalked off as an apparent, if not permanent, victory for the West over the East, Brokmeyer over Alcott —the stout heavyweight dialectician from Hardscrapple scoring at least a technical knockout over the welterweight seer from Spindle Hill.

III. EMERSON IN ST. LOUIS

In the meantime, the burly Brokmeyer and the acrid Snider notwithstanding, other Eastern luminaries went to St. Louis to shed and reflect light, but of them all only Emerson created any great stir in Old Philosophers' Row, when, the winter following Alcott's ill-starred visit of 1866, Harris imported the chief of the Transcendental diviners. The St. Louis Hegelians turned out *en masse* to meet the Concord sage—all but Brokmeyer. After his encounters with Alcott, he had enough of Yankee soothsayers, and contrived to keep his distance. Not so Harris, who was never more solicitous.

On one of his two visits to Alcott in Concord during the summer of 1865, Harris had met Emerson and had urged him to extend his next lecture tour to include St. Louis.[74] Emerson had previously improved several opportunities to learn something about Hegel, not the least of which had been his thumbing through a copy, hot from the press, of J. H. Stirling's *Secret of Hegel*. He had taken the book with him on his tour of the West during the winter of 1865-1866, had read it of nights in dingy, cheerless hotel rooms between the stages of his peregrinations, and had found it a "good book," offering "some lasting knowledge" and inviting him to "purer, loftier service," so that momentarily he felt himself lifted "quite out of prosaic surroundings."[75] But it is apparent that he lacked the capability or the will to follow Hegel in his technical arguments, for in the end he felt very much as he had a decade earlier when James E. Cabot had lent him some of Hegel's books: "I do not find my way into Hegel's works as readily as I had hoped, nor was I as richly rewarded as probably better scholars have been."[76] Nevertheless, he had kept an open mind and was willing, despite the rough treatment which Harris' men had meted out to Alcott, to go among them and to be set right if perchance they could show him what he had failed to find for himself. The opportunity presented a kind of challenge that Emerson was never the man to sidestep. So it came to pass that when he arrived in St. Louis on March 6, 1867,[77] he was prepared to listen but nonetheless careful not to be caught off guard, for he understood very well the epistemological chasm that separated St. Louis Hegelianism and Concord Transcendentalism, and he did not propose unwittingly to fall into it.

Harris having learned something during the protracted visit of Alcott the preceding winter, quartered Emerson in the old Lindell Hotel, whither four or five of his cohorts accompanied him to bid Emerson welcome.[78] Snider was among the number—but not Brokmeyer. Snider recalled the salutations and Emerson's willingness "generously to play with us a little while, but always at arm's length." He was "urbanely critical" and on his guard, for he knew himself to be in a nest of confirmed Hegelians. On their side, they instantly recognized him as made of firmer metal than Alcott; for the moment the introductory formalities were over, Snider observed, he took the offensive by "whipping out his rapier and . . . giving sly but very courtly digs at our Teutonic idol." "I cannot find," said Emerson, "any striking sentences in Hegel which I can take by themselves and quote. There is no period in him which rounds itself out into a detached thought, or pithy saying or rememberable metaphor . . . I always test an author by the number of single good things which I can catch up from his pages. When I fish in Hegel, I cannot get a bite; in addition the labor is so hard in reading him, that I get a headache."[79]

At the mention of a headache "the assembled philosophers smiled in chorus with the speaker," and Snider barely caught himself to avoid blurting out what was on the tip of his tongue: "Mr. Emerson, that may be the fault of the head, of the peculiar convolution of the brain." That would have made a decidedly bad beginning. It was bad enough as things were, for there developed an awkward pause, while Snider sighed for Brokmeyer to put this blasphemer in his place. Harris made ineffectual general conversation; then, warming up once more to philosophy and philosophers, he tried to get talk going again, but rather overdid the thing by running off into things remote and obscure, larding his talk with Hegelian nomenclature, until Emerson interrupted to say, "My preference is that the hideous skeleton of philosophy be covered with beautiful living tissue; I do not enjoy for my intellectual repast the dry bones of thought."[80]

Clearly Emerson was running away with the show, and Harris was playing right into his hands. Snider sighed again for Brokmeyer. His quills rose as he reflected, here is Mr. Emerson applying to us his own standard of writing and "seeking to Emersonize us." Surely, ruminated Snider, the implication is that we are on the wrong track, that it would be better for us to study Emerson than Hegel—though, of course, he doesn't exactly say that. But the implication is plain, and the sting is no less pointed because it isn't hammered home. Confessedly thin-skinned, Snider could contain himself no longer. Though he was the youngest of the set and knew himself to be "the greenest" for the business in hand, he dared to observe: "Mr. Emerson, you seem to deny the right of philosophy as a science to have its own distinctive terminology, as well as Mechanics and Chemistry. I judge that you regard the sole vehicle of thought as simply literary. But we hold that it must have its own well-defined terms, if it is ever to rise to its true scientific value."[81] And as he caught, or seemed to catch, "the beautiful stylists's . . . condescending smile of courteous contempt," he mustered enough audacity to lecture Emerson "with some degree of ardor," though perhaps not with the same degree that Brokmeyer might have applied had he been present: "It would seem impossible to organize philosophy into a system without its special nomenclature. The value of Hegel is his vast organization of thought; this is what we are seeking to appropriate, at least as a discipline. But in order to do so, we must learn to read his language, yea, learn to talk it also. Hegel has fine individual ideas, I think, scattered along on many a page, but these are only little stones which go to make the vast architecture of his philosophic temple. In other words, Hegel's system is what we are working so hard to master—his system of thought as an ideal construction of the universe."[82]

Of course, Snider, in his youthful self-conceit and ardent devotion to Hegel, could hardly have realized that Emerson knew all that—had known it ever since the early thirties when he had tried to get his thoughts on Nature in order; nor did Snider know that Emerson had found the method unsatisfactory, had lapsed back into an intuitional phase, and was only recently coming round to something approaching, though still far from identical with, the method which Snider was championing.[83]

Emerson let Snider's remarks pass. He was never one to disillusion a youthful idealist. Why should he quarrel with a young enthusiast over a method which he himself had repeatedly tried but failed to master? Yet one searches in vain in Emerson's journals and letters (or Alcott's, for that matter) for any reference to Snider. This silence is sufficiently conspicuous to suggest that Snider was in some measure *persona non grata* among the Concordians, as Snider himself sensed the situation later when he went, upon Harris' invitation, to give lectures in the Concord summer schools.[84] For his part, Snider did not learn until he went to Concord and more particularly when, more than a half-century later, he came to write his life of Emerson "what an awful goblin" he had conjured up by the use of that word *system*—"the horror of horrors, not only to him, but to his kindred Transcendentalists."[85]

Here it may be observed, in partial palliation of Snider, that when he published his biography of Emerson in 1921, he not only wrote a sympathetic and illuminating interpretation but was among the first to utilize fully the then newly published *Journals* of Emerson as an indispensable fund of information illustrating the evolution of the Emersonian philosophy. To be sure, James E. Cabot had anticipated him in the exploration of these rich resources in his biography of Emerson which appeared in 1887; but he had worked under the handicap of examining the journals while they were still in manuscript form and in a relatively chaotic state of organization. Oscar W. Firkins was the first to whom the ten volumes of printed notebooks were available, but his study of Emerson, despite the excellence of its presentation of Emerson's literary personality, is markedly faulty in its attempt to reconstruct the course of Emerson's thinking. His account of Emerson's philosophical development becomes involved in all manner of convolutions and terminological difficulties, where Snider's interpretation is straightforward, clear, and consistent.

Back to Emerson and the welcoming committee at the old Lindell Hotel. Following Snider's little lecture, Harris was observed to have a bad time of it.

He was visibly ill at ease. Things were going badly. He lapsed into self-occupied, Sphinx-like silence, for he dared not speak on one side or the other. From that moment the suspicion grew that Harris, the only Yankee among them, was angling in strange waters; a dozen years later the St. Louisans had their suspicions confirmed when he grasped the first good opportunity that came to return to his native New England rocks.[86] Snider, left alone to fence with this mighty New Englander, felt unequal to the task. All he could do was to repeat internally, "Oh, for just ten minutes of Brokmeyer at his best," for assuredly Mr. Emerson would then hear "some of his much-desired pithy sentences white-hot in their creative glow and enwrapped in a metaphorical tornado which would have whirled him off his feet. He might appreciate it [mused Snider], but probably would not; for Mr. Emerson had little of the Titanic or of the Demonic in him, though he seemed once to recognize applaudingly some such quality in Walt Whitman."[87]

Harris invited Emerson to his home, where he read him some of his own productions, notably the one on Raphael's Transfiguration, soon to be published in the first number of the *Journal of Speculative Philosophy*.[88] On its appearance in print, Emerson, by then back in Concord, wrote to thank Harris for sending the copy that contained it, as well as for "the advance sheets" of the second number of the *Journal;* and what was much to the point, he inclosed $2.00 for his subscription.[89]

For the rest of his stay in St. Louis, little is known about it. None of the members of the Society recorded anything specific regarding the lectures of Emerson's before their group. Presumably, on this first visit, the Society contented itself with formally sponsoring his lecture on "American Culture" on the Public School Library course.[90] Indeed, it seems that he remained no longer than a day or two in the city. Yet he continued to demonstrate some enthusiasm for Harris and his men and reported to Henry James, Sr., "It was a true gratification to see Harris at St. Louis midst his German Atheists, & to share his pleasure in that, though he had begun alone, he now counted . . . nineteen young men as spiritual and affirmative philosophers, & could rely on them as active propagandists."[91] He maintained an "auxiliary" membership[92] in the Society and became a regular subscriber and presumably a reader of the *Journal.* Harris continued to send advance sheets of the first numbers, which were especially detailed in setting forth the aims of the St. Louis school and abundant in Hegelian materials, both translation and explanation. He complimented Harris upon his "brave undertaking," and added, "I shall think better than ever of my countrymen if they shall sustain it. I mean that you shall make me acquainted with the true value & performance of Hegel, who, at first sight is not engaging nor at second sight satisfying. But his immense fame cannot be mistaken, and I shall read & wait."[93]

Henceforth, until Harris himself settled in Concord, there was a steady interchange of letters and opinions between Emerson and Harris: they borrowed each other's books, they pooled their efforts and influence to secure literary and academic advancement for J. H. Stirling, the Scotch Hegelian, and they consulted together regarding contributions and editorial policies for the *Journal*.[94] Emerson steadily encouraged Harris' journalistic venture and insisted on paying for his copy of the *Journal of Speculative Philosophy*, although Harris had sent it gratis. Apparently Harris confided to Emerson, as early as 1870, his ambition to bring Hegel to Concord, for Emerson wrote, on March 3, 1870: "We have no news yet to give you of real progress in speculative philosophy in Mass*tts*. It is a good sign surely of the courage of our new President at Cambridge in establishing University Lectures; and he is this year making a direct attempt to bring Mr. Stirling from Edinburgh. I think it is good that Mr. J. E. Cabot reads lectures in these weeks on Kant. The class are very small. It was a mistake to make the price of admission too high. I have put my three vols. of the 'Journal' to be bound and mean to read them much in the next month. Thanks especially for Hegel in No. 12, and for Mr. Davidson's 'Parmenides.' This last is a wonderful piece of Greek precocity."[95]

The "Hegel in No. 12" for which Emerson thanked Harris is a reference to the latter's translation in no. 1 of vol. I from Hegel's "Philosophische Propaedeutik," which the translator entitled "The Science of Rights, Morals, and Religion." Lacking decisive evidence regarding how long Emerson continued to read Harris' publication, we are unable to conjecture how much he derived from that source. But if he read no further than vol. IV, no. 1 (March, 1870), he became exposed to more than a mere smattering of German speculation; if he continued to read, and comprehend, subsequent numbers, he stood an excellent chance to become one of the best informed Americans of his time on the subject of German metaphysics. That he did become thus informed is improbable.

But the fact that he had the first three volumes of the *Journal of Speculative Philosophy* put in permanent bindings indicates that he valued their contents; the resolution formed on March 3, 1870, "to read them much in the next month" (presumably in preparation for his Harvard lectures on the natural history of intellect, to be delivered during April and May) seems significant. If he kept the resolution and read, then or later, the contents of the first twelve numbers, he became acquainted with a remarkable body of information on German systems of thought, for they included, among other provocative essays, Harris' smashing twenty-page attack upon the entire Spencerian dispensation. Kroeger's translation of Fichte's *Science of Knowledge,* several expository articles on Kant's system of critical transcendentalism (including Kroeger's very excellent essay in vol. III), Thomas Davidson's translation of Schelling's "Introduction to the Philosophy of Nature," Bernard's analysis of Hegel's "Aesthetics," Harris' essay on "Hegel's First Principle," and his translations from the *Phenomenology* and the *Logic,* together with articles on Leibnitz, Winckelmann, Swedenborg, Cousin, Berkeley, Schopenhauer, and notably on Goethe.

In the absence of precisely demonstrable influence of these materials upon Emerson's subsequent works, the conclusion must be that while he may have made good his resolution, his reading of the *Journal* did not affect him vitally. Much of it was highly technical, and quite probably his old aversion to the technicalities of metaphysics revived. The conclusion seems to be that now, as earlier, he divined the general import of Hegel and his compeers, but that he contented himself with grasping the general significance of Hegelianism without plumbing the metaphysical depths or acquiring the dialectical proficiency requisite for a detailed comprehension and a complete assimilation.

In 1879 the Concord School of Philosophy was established, with Alcott as the titular, and Harris the real, head. Henceforth there was an abundance of talk in Concord about Hegel, with Harris most diligent to do the work of the master, and Alcott, too, lending a hand occasionally, as when he tried to expound Kant (to the satisfaction of no one) during the Kant Centennial of the third session.[96] Even Emerson joined the School; and though he did not undertake to talk about Hegel, he delivered two lectures—one on "Aristocracy" and another, ironically enough, on "Memory."[97] By this time Emerson's memory was failing, and his mind was wandering. Whatever their impact on others was to be, Harris and his Western Hegelians settled Concord too late to be of much use to Emerson.

IV. The Extension of Hegelianism

These contents and conflicts between New England intuitionalism and St. Louis rationalism are symptomatic of other divergences, antagonisms, and cross-purposes that characterized the several idealistic movements of the last century. As we focus our attention upon the liberalism of the East, we become aware that Unitarianism, Transcendentalism, the Free

Religious Association, and the Radical Club, for example, were at once opposed to each other in some phases, yet united under the same banner by which the idealism of one is recognizable as not radically different from that of the others, but rather representing successive extensions or progressions of the same basic spirit or impulse. Similarly, when we turn to the West, we are struck by an even greater multiplicity and diversity of effort that stemmed nevertheless from the same base. In St. Louis, for instance, during the three decades following the Civil War, there were enough clubs, societies, and organizations—often drawing upon the same clientele—for them to have devoured each other. Aside from the Hegel Club, which was founded shortly after the close of the War, and which engendered the Philosophical Society, there was the Kant Club[98] from about 1874 to 1890, which met every Saturday night, and the Aristotle Club, founded by Thomas Davidson about 1873[99]—not to mention circles and classes of cultivated women, who were not admitted to the Philosophical Society, but who found these less formal organizations suited to their needs for partaking of the philosophical ferment of the city, for leaders like Harris, Snider, Davidson, Cook, Kroeger, and Holland went a constant round among them.

More or less closely associated with these philosophical groups were the several literary clubs, the prime mover behind most of which was Snider. Among the more long-lived was the Shakespeare Society, established in 1870, by Amelia C. Fruchte. Originally a study club dedicated to a consideration of Snider's Hegelian interpretation of Shakespeare, it also studied *seriatim* Snider's other "Bibles"— Homer, Dante, and Goethe. Even after it became a social club, in which form it survived until 1916, Snider found in this group the nucleus for many of his Literary Schools, and he developed lieutenants, such as Mrs. Thomas E. Ferguson and William F. Woerner, from among their number who carried on while he was away, as he often was for years. Dr. Holland's Literary Club, also associated with the Sniderian literary renaissance, took a theological turn. Nor were the arts neglected. Harris' "Musical Evenings," once a week, effected an introduction of Beethoven, Mozart, Schumann, and Mendelssohn in circles beyond the Germans and German-Americans of St. Louis. An art club, founded during the War and originally an informal discussion group, soon blossomed forth as the "Art Society," holding semi-public lectures, exhibitions, and discussions on sculpture, painting, music, and literature. The quality of the Society can be gauged by the type of papers to which it listened, such as Harris' essay on "Raphael's Transfiguration," or Davidson's "Parmenides," both subsequently printed in the *Journal of Speculative Philosophy.* Much more closely identified than they would be today with all these were the several educational institutes and federations of teachers, notably the St. Louis Froebel Society, the Society of Pedagogy, the Teachers' Fellowship Society, and the Wednesday Club.

This extraordinary organizational activity, to say nothing of the divergence of points of view and of objectives, would under ordinary circumstances have provided a perfect setting for the St. Louis enthusiasts to talk themselves and their societies to death. But nothing like that happened. Keeping in mind Emerson's words about the necessity of being at once Knowers, Sayers, and Doers, they particularly heeded the command of their triune leadership—Brokmeyer, Harris, and Snider — who agreed that their first duty was to realize their self-activity in expression, in short, *to publish.* The persistence with which they held to this purpose may be measured by upwards of a thousand titles that issued from this group of Hegel-inspired St. Louisans.

While these multiform activities might suggest that the St. Louis Movement was local in its scope, the truth is that it was from the first ambitious to achieve national influence. It remained rooted in St. Louis, but wherever and whenever an occasion arose for a St. Louisan to carry the light into the provinces, east or west, north or south, he accepted the challenge. Not one of them was a *Kleinwinkel;* and when, in 1921, a commemorative meeting was held on the occasion of Snider's eightieth birthday, Lewis J. Block said with some justice that to call the Movement the "St. Louis" Movement represented a diminution of its true scope and influence—that it belonged "organically and properly to the entire history of philosophic thought in the United States."[100]

Aside from Snider's far-flung operations, Brokmeyer's distant sorties, and Harris' numerous appearances in many places and capacities,[101] there were men and women, resident in other cities and communities who organized philosophical societies of their own that came, in one way or another, within the orbit of the St. Louis Movement. Among the more influential of those in the West was the Plato Club, soon to be renamed the Akademe, founded by Dr. Hiram K. Jones at Jacksonville, Illinois, "The Athens of the West."[102] Co-founder of the Microscopic Society, a charter member of the Literary Society, founder and president of the Jacksonville Historical Society, professor of physiology and of philosophy at Illinois College, founder of the Plato Club in 1865, of the American Akademe about 1884, and the motivating power behind the *Journal of the American Akademe* (1884-1892), Dr. Jones was literally omnipresent and became for Jacksonville what Brokmeyer, Harris, and Snider combined were for St. Louis. While this group drew its basic inspiration from Plato, the addition of Lewis J. Block and David H. Harris (brother of William Torrey) during the early seventies infused a large element of Hegelianism and prevented the group from developing a too esoteric Platonism.[103] While the Plato Club remained largely a Jacksonville institution, it attracted many notable visitors and members from such cities as Quincy, Decatur, and Bloomington, Illinois; Osceola, Missouri; Davenport, Iowa; and, of course, St. Louis, as well as Chicago. It also sought stimulation from abroad: Thomas H. Johnson of Osceola, S. H. Emery of Quincy, and Horace Hills Morgan, editor of *The Western,* came repeatedly; Snider talked to the Illinois Platonists about Hegel, Shakespeare, and Goethe; Thomas Davidson, about Aristotle; W. T. Harris, about Hegel; Alcott came to hold "Conversations," and Emerson, to lecture. Its membership included people from England, Australia, France, Mexico, and virtually every State in the Union, so that Jones had some justification for declaring, "This is not a local but a continental association."[104] Although the Jacksonville contingent withdrew, after three or four years, from the Concord School of Philosophy, without their active support in the beginning the School could hardly have been established.

St. Louis and Jacksonville, the two leading centers

of Philosophical activity in the Midwest during the second half of the nineteenth century, were rivals in the sense that the former was as largely inspired by Hegel as the latter was by Plato; yet their efforts were often coördinated and sometimes unified. Both exerted influence in spheres that diverged and then drew together again. Thus, the St. Louis School projected itself most clearly in the ferment which Snider and his colleagues created in Chicago, at the same time that it injected its pedagogical philosophy into the experimental normal schools at Kirksville, Missouri, and Terre Haute, Indiana. Meanwhile the Platonists of Jacksonville inspired perhaps smaller but no less enthusiastic groups of disciples in Osceola, Decatur, Bloomington, and Quincy. But eventually all found a common meeting ground in the Concord School of Philosophy, whither all gravitated in 1879.

Osceola as a center of activity for idealistic philosophy, under the direction of Thomas H. Johnson, never achieved the closely-unified organization attained by Jones' Akademe, partly because it concerned itself less with following closely Plato or any other single philosopher than with the historical study of the idealistic tradition of thought, and partly because it found its chief activity less in organizational forms than in Johnson's journalistic efforts as editor of *The Platonist* (1881-1888) and *The Bibliotheca Platonica* (1889-1890) to extend the influence alike of the St. Louis, the Jacksonville, and its own idealists. Johnson, as editor, historical scholar, and bibliophile, did notable work and collected a library of idealist literature at Osceola that surpassed every other private collection in the country. Osceola, Quincy, Jacksonville, and St. Louis formed the four nuclear points among which there was kept up a steady exchange of papers and a constant round of visitation. They formed a circuit which Easterners like Emerson and Alcott did not neglect to cover in their "hemisphere belting" tours.

The fourth group in this circuit was the Friends in Council, founded in 1866 at Quincy, under the joint leadership of Mrs. Sarah Denman and Samuel H. Emery.[105] As among the Platonists of Jacksonville, their original inspiration came from the Platonic tradition, but they made all learning their province from the beginning. Like the Jacksonville Akademe, they were "a School rather than a sect in philosophy."[106] Like them, too, they attracted a large number of out-of-town members. As Emery's influence increased, Mrs. Denman took charge of the literary part of the programs, while Emery led the group more and more in the direction of Hegel. He bought Hegel's works in the original; but, unable to trust his own ability as a translator, borrowed from Harris a copy of Brokmeyer's translation of the *Logic* and had a typewritten copy prepared. This was completed by 1875 and became the standard source of reference for the group. By March of 1878 he had persuaded Dr. Jones to study Hegel, and at Dr. Jones' request another copy was struck off. When, the next year, accompanied by Edward McClure, he went east to study in the Harvard Law School and to become the Director of the Concord School, Emery took his manuscript translation, in three large volumes, with him, so that his copy and another which Harris brought were used to good purpose throughout the Concord sessions. In Concord they had better luck than Emery had in his efforts to indoctrinate Boston and to turn philosophical discussion in Cambridge toward Hegel. Years later William James recalled going over, with James E. Cabot, C. C. Everett, Tom Davidson, and others who formed a "little" philosophical club, " a good part of Hegel's larger *Logic*, under the self-constituted leadership of two young business men from Illinois, who had become enthusiastic Hegelians and, knowing almost no German, had actually possessed themselves of a manuscript translation of the entire three volumes of Logic, made by an extraordinary Pomeranian [*sic*] immigrant, named Brockmeyer [*sic*]. These disciples were leaving business for the law and studying at the Harvard law-school; but they saw the whole universe through Hegelian spectacles, and a more admirable *homo unius libri* than one of them, with his three big folios of Hegelian manuscript, I have never had the good fortune to know."[107]

V. THE DISPERSION OF THE FORCES

In the meantime the dialectics of individualism in St. Louis had begun to work. The Philosophical Society, despite the fact that it engendered a thousand books and the first journal of speculative philosophy worthy of the name in the English language, never achieved a close organization. On first consideration this amorphism appears odd because, unlike the Transcendental Club, which grew out of a very informal discussion and never rallied round anything so definite as a great book or a single saint, but preserved to the end a whole galaxy of high-priests from Confucius to Emerson himself, the Philosophical Society was acknowledged by its founders to have had its "original source of inspiration . . . in Brokmeyer's translation of Hegel's Logic." But this book came to be a veritable "Book of Fate, destined to stay unborn in the unprinted underworld during the whole life of the St. Louis Movement."[108] So long as Brokmeyer was among them, he gave the membership unity; but when, bent on "self-determination," he left them to follow his own daemon, the Movement fell apart. Each one as a super-individualist, began to exercise "self-activity" and to follow his "Super-Vocation," according to

Brokmeyer's prescription. Harris found himself first as editor of the *Journal of Speculative Philosophy;* then he turned to journalism, the lecture platform, and the Concord School of Philosophy, and finally to the administration of the office of public instruction in Washington.

Snider was the next to strike out on his own. As soon as he had attained a certain mastery of Hegel —"at least [he says] disentanglement from the vortical labyrinth of ever-spinning and interlacing triplets of categories" to the point where "I could spin them better than they could spin me"[109]—he entered upon the pursuit of his career as "A Writer of Books" though it meant keeping close company with "Chum Poverty."[110] He was active in many directions—as an Hegelian expositor of the Four Great Literary Bibles in four bulky commentaries; as a teacher of classes in Homer, Shakespeare, Dante, and Goethe in St. Louis and Chicago; as a lecturer in a region embracing St. Louis, Baltimore, Concord, and Milwaukee; as a "professor" in the Chicago Kindergarten College; as the founder of the Communal University in both Chicago (1887-1895) and St. Louis (after 1895); as the originator of the Sniderian psychology (expounded in ten volumes between 1896 and 1905); as the conductor of the Goethe School in Milwaukee; and as a lecturer in five of the Concord summer schools. In all of these pursuits his personal influence was often profound and generally pervasive, while his books published his creed even more generally. Yet throughout his long career, he made it always perfectly plain that he spoke for himself alone, and that, above all else, he wanted to keep his individualism inviolate. The St. Louis Movement, if it wished to come his way, would be welcome; but he would not accommodate his plans merely to keep a movement alive.

Tom Davidson, though he had drawn his inspiration during the sixties from the same "University Brokmeyer"[111] that had animated Harris and Snider, was always "a jolly drifter and general free fighter"[112] who delighted as much "to kick over the traces as to help pull the load."[113] He early developed interests tangential to the Movement by professing usually Aristotle in favor of Hegel, berating modern Christianity while confessing himself a classic heathen, and playing to perfection the part of the *advocatus diaboli*, eventually turning even upon Greek culture with what Snider called "damnatory bitterness." Upon leaving St. Louis in 1875, he became, as the London *Spectator* said, "the last of the Wandering Scholars," primarily interested in Greek and Roman antiquities, but returning often to the United States to support or confuse the plans of the Concord, Milwaukee, St. Louis, or Chicago schools. After 1887 he established, in association

with the People's Institute and the Education Alliance
of New York and with the help of Joseph Pulitzer,
the Bread-Winners' College for a group of eager
young men recruited chiefly from among Jewish
socialists of the lower East Side. Soon thereafter he
sought a retreat, first at Farmington, Connecticut,
where he organized a summer school for his pupils,
and later, on a farm in the more remote regions of
Glenmore in the Adirondacks. Here, beginning in
1889, he provided for his young East-Siders, who
were bent on social renovation and cultural acquisition, and for all cultists who cared to share his lavish
hospitality, an elaborate array of lecturers, including
himself, Percival Chubb, Mary C. McCulloch, William Torrey Harris, Amelia C. Fruchte (all of whom
had St. Louis connections), but also people like
Henry Gardiner, Josiah Royce, William James, and
John Dewey.[114] Thither came, too, Platonists from
Osceola, Hegelians from Chicago and Quincy, and
several members of the Jacksonville Akademe. Thus
were brought together, in remote Glenmore, under
the aegis of the brilliant, militant, mercurial, Scotch-
born Davidson, whom William James dubbed "The
Knight-Errant of the Intellectual Life,"[115] both
Jew and Gentile—Hegelians from St. Louis and
Quincy, Platonists from Jacksonville and Osceola,
Sniderian psychologists from Chicago and St. Louis,
Transcendentalists from Concord and Boston, and

the professional philosophers from the academic halls.

Meanwhile, back in St. Louis, the leadership had devolved on the shoulders of men like Kroeger and Woerner who had their business or profession to attend to, or upon women like Susan B. Blow and Amelia C. Fruchte, who, however capable in their own spheres, were women, who had never been within the inner circle of the original group, and who, for one reason or another, were unable to take over where Brokmeyer, Harris, and Snider had left off. Thus the Movement as a movement lost force, even while the individuals that had once formed it went on with unabated vigor to prosecute its work, each one as he happened to conceive it.

While the idealistic movement in the West was thus beginning to manifest unmistakable signs of disintegration, a momentary gleam of hope that all might yet be saved came in the form of the Concord School of Philosophy whither all turned hopefully in 1879. The Concord School is often rated as the most influential, as it probably was, of the idealistic movements of the late nineteenth century. It is also sometimes considered as merely a recrudescence of Platonism on Puritan soil, or simply as a resurrection of earlier New England Transcendentalism. It was more than either, for without the support of Western Hegelianism, the Concord institution could never have got beyond the conceptual stage in Alcott's mind. Dean Alcott, without Emery, Jones, and Harris, and the "students" they brought in their wake, would have had the title but little more. The entire movement is more properly viewed as a cyclic development, which, beginning as New England Transcendentalism in the thirties and forties, partially begot or reinforced during the next decades the Hegelian movement in St. Louis; both combined to fructify the smaller outposts of idealistic thought in Jacksonville, Quincy, and Osceola in the West; finally, during the seventies and eighties, when all the Western groups—Platonic and Hegelian—headed for Concord to join the Eastern idealists in the formation of the Concord School, the movement came round full circle.

VI. The Convergence Toward Concord

As early as 1840 Amos Bronson Alcott had conceived the idea of an academe or "university" with himself, Ripley, Hedge, Parker, and "one or two others . . . to make a puissant faculty."[116] He carried the idea in his head for many years. His friend Emerson, it was well known, cared little for "schools." Although both were struck forcibly by the followings which Harris in St. Louis and Jones in Jacksonville had built for themselves, nothing constructive and practical was done in Concord until

1878, when Emerson was past caring one way or the other. Then it was, in the summer of that year, that Hiram K. Jones, accompanied by his wife, Mr. and Mrs. Elizur Wolcott, Mr. and Mrs. Mathew B. Denman (of Quincy), and two or three other "Westerners"[117] came to Concord. After "a fortnight of glorious talk," Jones and his party left for their homes. "The Concord School was assured."[118]

It is significant that Jones the Platonist and not Harris the Hegelian was the co-founder of the Concord School of Philosophy. Jones and Alcott originally envisaged the school as a Platonic institution. That Hegel soon disputed the realm of Plato is a circumstance which Alcott would hardly have welcomed in 1878, for he was, in spite of the numerous other philosophic currents with which he had come in contact, still predominantly a Platonist. But Harris had been too long a fellow conspirator with him in the aim to found a school in Concord to be excluded, now that the plan was materializing. What is more, once Harris was invited to participate, the die was cast. Hegel, along with Harris, rapidly gained the ascendancy. However much Jones gesticulated and Alcott regretted the "purely speculative," Hegel rose in power in direct proportion as Harris gained control of the academe.

The school got off to an auspicious start. The several lieutenants in various parts of the country whipped up enthusiasm. Though the School opened on July 15, 1879, "without funds," it almost paid its way even the first year. Lecturers were paid $10 for each discourse; outsiders like Professor Peirce were given, in addition, especial "thanks for the entertainment and instruction." Thus Sanborn, as Treasurer, cast up receipts of $733 against expenses of $739, and closed the books of the first year by supplying the deficit out of his own pocket. Early in 1880, Mrs. Elizabeth Thompson of New York donated $1,000 to the cause. After the Hillside Chapel was built, there remained $673, which served "to secure the School from risk . . . to keep the Chapel in repair, and to increase the furniture." However, this balance was ultimately whittled down by the increase of the lecturer's fee from $10 to $15. Even so, Sanborn estimated that the School would have ended with a substantial amount in the treasury if they had not given away "many tickets each year." As it was, the balance in 1888 was thirty-one cents, which, says Sanborn, he pocketed, without compunction, "as his salary for ten years."[119]

The first school lasted six weeks, eleven lectures being given each week;[120] the next two schools ran for five weeks, eleven lectures to the week.[121] During 1882, 1883, and 1884, the sessions were shortened to four weeks, ten lectures a week;[122] in 1885, the school ran for three weeks;[123] thereafter it varied from two to three weeks.[124]

The first school opened, says Alcott, "with a full attendance."[125] After Mr. Emery's "genial welcome of our visitors," Alcott took the floor to present "an outline of our method of communication and the spirit of our purpose," which he explained is "to pursue the path of speculative philosophy . . . the lectures serving mainly as a text for discussion," though "dispute and polemical debate" are to be avoided. Mrs. Cheney read two lectures on art. Next, Harris lectured on "the presuppositions which imply and, logically follow, conduct of Personality, and are the sum and substance of all thinking." Here already Alcott confessed having some trouble "following the steps" by which Harris reached his conclusions; but the Rev. Dr. Kedney, Dr. Hiram K. Jones, and Professors Andrews and Beers of Yale, with several of the students, took an "eager part in questioning and discussing the subject." That same evening Emery, Harris, Jones, Kedney, and McClure discussed further "the Hegelian Idea and methods." Thus the Concord School got off to a start under Hegelian auspices which Alcott, if he had had his way about it, would have modified to make the method less speculative—so as to treat "imagination, reason, and conscience in its threefold attributes as one and entire, thus speaking to the reason and faith at once." This method, he believed would reach "the many," while the method of Harris obviously would affect "but the few."[126]

Accordingly Alcott lectured the next day on psychology as the key to all knowledge, taking care to make his discourse a "stairway" or introduction that should be more intelligible to all the company than Harris' subtle metaphysics were likely to be.[127] The day following Dr. Jones initiated his series of ten lectures on Plato. His first discourse dealt with "the Platonic significance of ideas," and Alcott observed that his "forcible manner and novelty of thought interest and provoke eager discussion." In the afternoon Harris resumed "his exposition of the speculative method." "His auditors," continued Alcott, "admire, wonder at the subtlety of his expositions and are apparently persuaded of his holding the key to the absolute truth of things, both in matter and mind. The faith he inspires is almost universal, though none, it may be, comprehend [*sic*] his method completely."[128] Between the two it was hard to choose. Jones' "allegorical genius" was "refreshing;" yet Alcott was forced "sometimes to question whether the Platonic ideas are not modified essentially by the Doctor's exposition." Then, too, such a remark as Higginson's, that "the defect of the Transcendental School is want of form" was a little disturbing.[129]

Moreover, Jones, though he had disciples who

would have heard him all day, lacked the virtue of condensation; his lectures had virtually no terminal facilities; and some of his listeners found five hours of his lecturing so tiring on the mind that they were forced occasionally to go out for fresh air.[130] "Sometimes, indeed [so it was reported in Boston], an irreverant couple would leave these Platonic expositions of the 'physical sensorium' and 'spiritual sensoria' and be off for an hour's row on the Concord River . . . but as the lectures of Dr. Jones were, like the quality of Japanese pictures, such as would permit approach from any angle of vision,—upside down, or divided anywhere; any part, despite mathematical laws, being equal to the whole,—they lent themselves to the charming possibilities of being taken in sections. Indeed the irreverent and unplatonic mind was not infrequently found to insist that a part was better than the whole of the good doctor's discourses, whose length suggested the infinite leisure of the Eternities rather than the limits of an ephemeral summer's day."[131]

The Illinois Platonist was used to holding the center of the stage and delivering his opinions *ex cathedra*. Harris, brought up in the school of Brokmeyer, was used to the give-and-take method of trading arguments. He might lecture for an hour or more, but his discourses inspired questions, and his manner encouraged discussion, which often ran for an hour and a half, even two hours, beyond the appointed time.[132] As the meetings went on, Alcott continued to prefer the analogical method by which reason and imagination were brought into play jointly;[133] but he began to perceive that though Jones was being heard with deep interest,[134] the interest provoked by Harris seemed somehow to have a more substantial quality.

"Mr. Harris lectures to a crowded company on 'Immortality.' As usual, his arguments are profoundly logical and abstruse, but he is heard with unbroken attention and interest. His lectures are awakening a novel interest in the subjects he treats, and his audiences increase in numbers from day to day. Such consecutive and convincing statements on themes so subtle and spiritual have seldom been treated with like clearness and conclusiveness."[135]

By July 25, Jones was lecturing on the "Apology of Socrates" to "a smaller but interested audience,"[136] while Harris, speaking on "methods of study" and recommending "Kant's Critique of Pure Reason particularly" as a whetstone of the mind, held a "large" audience.[137] Harris emerged from the first school having on the whole "the larger audiences."[138] On August 4, for example, Jones' discourse on "Plato's doctrine of Reminiscence and Preexistence" presented, says Alcott, "a doctrine too remote from our accepted modes of thinking to be rendered intelligible at once," and hence "many questions were asked and further illustration is needed to satisfy some of the questioners."[139] That same night Alcott observed that Harris, speaking at the Orthodox Vestry, on the "relation of Art, Science and Religion to Philosophy, or the Prime of Theology," had "a full audience and interests as heretofore," and "won general acceptance from all who have heard him speak." "Philosophy is sure in his treatment," added Alcott, "to be the most practical and precious acquisition, one with life and the reason of things."[140]

For the remainder of the session, Alcott conversed on his favorite doctrine of "Lapse" and "Atonement," Mrs. Cheney read papers on "Art," Blake read extracts from Thoreau's journals, Jones on "the Body, Spiritual and Natural" and on "Platonic Ideals," Sanborn on "Social Science," Bartol on "Education," and Elizabeth Palmer Peabody had her say about women's rights.[141] Alcott delivered the valedictory of mutual congratulation on August 16, on which day he wrote in his diary, "The School closed happily." The continuance of the Concord School of Philosophy was assured.[142]

The first Concord school was truly introductory, the whole range of human intellectual, artistic, and social interests having been covered. Subsequent sessions were more specialized. That of 1880 already showed some evidence of planned specialization:

the hand of Harris is unmistakable in the planning. David A. Wasson lectured on "The Philosophy of History," Harris himself on "The History of Philosophy," Sanborn on "The Philosophy of Charity," John S. Kedney on "The Philosophy of the Sublime and the Beautiful," and Snider on "The Philosophy of Shakespeare," while Jones and Harris continued their unscheduled but nonetheless real debate on "The Platonic Philosophy" *versus* "The Speculative Philosophy," and Alcott served as moderator at the same time that he held five conversations on "Mysticism," supplemented by four lectures by W. H. Channing on the same subject.[143]

The third (1881) session continued with Harris and Jones as the protagonists, each with his customary two courses (each one comprising five lectures) on Hegel and on Plato, respectively. Two innovations are notable. First, Snider's lectures on Shakespeare had been so successful the preceding year that he was asked to enlarge the literary content of the school by discoursing on "Greek Life and Literature," a subject of which he was full so shortly after his return from Athens and Rome. Second, the centennial of Kant's *Critique of Pure Reason* was observed by seven lecturers on Kant, August 2 to 6.[144] The participants in this most distinctive feature of the third school were Mrs. Julia Ward Howe, Rev. C. A. Bartol, Mr. J. E. Cabot, Presidents Noah

Porter of Yale and John Bascom of Wisconsin, and Professors F. H. Hedge, George S. Morris, J. W. Mears, and John Watson. Secretary Sanborn reported, in the number of the *Journal of Speculative Philosophy* for July, 1881, the lectures and the discussions held on August 6, the day set aside for exclusive devotion to the Kant Centennial. Of all the published reports, this one is, within its limits, the most informative and revelatory of the temper of the Concord Faculty at the time with reference to critical transcendentalism.

Mrs. Julia Ward Howe opened the celebration with an original poem, "On Leaving for a Time the Study of Kant," and a brief discussion of "The Results of Kant"; whereupon Rev. J. S. Kedney read President Porter's paper on "The Relation of Kant's Philosophy to Ethics and Religion." When Mrs. Howe, observing that Kant had marked out the domains of religion and philosophy as separate, objected to Noah Porter's bringing the two "too much together," Samuel Emery wanted to know whether she understood that Kant, in the *Critique of Practical Reason*, "did not intend to consider questions of theology?" Her answer, that "the effort required to follow such a discourse" as Porter's did not leave one "able to do much in criticizing it afterwards," was considered unsatisfactory; and Dr. Jones felt himself called upon to add that "Kant's conclusions,

Kant's philosophy does not matter," but "his method, his process of thinking, does." "Neither Aristotle, nor Plato, nor Kant, nor Schelling, nor Hegel is to be looked to as having spoken the last word, as having given us the consummation of philosophic thought." No, Kant's "greatness as a philosopher appears in the fact that he raised to view the never-ended problems of human life and human society, that his *thinking* is his philosophy; not his *result* of thinking, but his thinking itself."[145]

At this point Alcott interposed his views of the distinction between the pure reason and the practical reason. His remarks illustrate the over-simplification of Kant which was common among his transcendental brethren, and explain why some (Alcott, for example) failed to grasp the import of the Kantian criticism, while others (such as Emerson and Parker) understood the general significance of the Kantian epistemology but gave the wrong explanations of how and why the distinctions helped Kant to his conclusions. "In the first treatise," says Alcott, Kant tried "to explore the possibilities, the reach of the pure reason, or the reason unilluminated by faith, or, by what he called the 'categorical imperative,' the conscience. So I will take these two terms—reason and conscience—as expressing, in a generalized form, the two phases of Kant's thinking." It is hard to imagine Harris sitting through this "generalized" explanation of the Kantian criticism without wincing. What might have happened at this juncture if Brokmeyer had been present is interesting to speculate upon. But Harris and ~~Snider~~ Brokmeyer had previously settled between them the question of whether Brokmeyer should be invited to Concord by deciding emphatically, "It cannot be done, it cannot be done! . . . he would be sure to spill over in some diablery, or even profanity, which would shock all New England." The newspapers, they decided, had already quite enough to caricature without Brokmeyer's contributing any choice morsels.[146]

Alcott went on in his exposition: "In the first treatise he [Kant] does not seem to have taken into his thought what he called the Practical Reason in the other; he uses 'reason' in two senses. But really does he not mean faith, or the necessary influence which the affections have upon reason? He finds in this first treatise that the reason cannot solve moral questions . . . he becomes confused because he is seeking to find depths by the pure reason which of itself it cannot fathom. He finds he can come to no sure conclusions, and he ends in the unknowable, and must be classed as an agnostic with Spencer and Huxley and all that class. The Free Religionists largely, and even Unitarians to some extent, appear to have fallen into that error, and may quote Kant as authority."[147]

Here it may be observed (1) that Alcott paid scant attention to Kant's careful distinctions between *a posteriori* and *a priori* methods, (2) that he had not an inkling of Kant's differentiation between the regulative and the constitutive aspects of the reason, and (3) that his easy identification of Kant with Huxley in method, and of practical reason with conscience and faith, without reference to whether they proceed *a posteriori* or *a priori,* involves misconceptions not only of the Kantian distinction between understanding and reason but also of the distinction between pure and practical reason.

Alcott proceeded to explain: "thus he [Kant] settles nothing satisfactorily. He merely shows the infirmity of reason by itself. Then taking it up again in his Practical treatise, he speaks of the Categorical Imperative. 'You ought,' he says . . . There is something more in that 'ought' than in pure reason. Pure reason is not sufficient. The conscience, the moral sentiment, ascends above it. All that we can do is to strive to find it, to find in the conscience the voice of God, the Holy Spirit descending and taking possession of the human soul, and thus empowering the reason to make new discoveries, extend its horizon wider and wider under the illumination, the inspiration of faith."

At this point Harris might well have interrupted to remind Alcott of Kant's distinction between *"transcendant* illusions" and *"transcendental* knowledge," but Harris was not one to cross Alcott or to bring his Dean into ridicule. So Alcott went on—

"Now, putting these two facts [*sic*] together—conscience and reason—and trying to find a term which will express all that can be thus received and conceived, we say *revelation*. For, unless a revelation is made to the heart, the love in us, and also to the reason through the moral sentiment, revelation is incomplete; it is but a doctrine, a dogma."[148]

Professing to treat Kant "with all hospitality," he likens him to "a Columbus exploring unknown regions"; "Kant is an explorer; he goes on to unfold relations, and tells us, with an absolute honesty of conviction, what he saw, and no more. When he saw anything, he has reported it to us; and when he put out his sounding-lines and brought up nothing, he said so. Is not that what he said, this Columbus? That is the man we are here celebrating in this chapel." Here we have a perfect example of Alcott's favorite type of "analogical" reasoning,—"the pure truth of the poet interblending imagination and reason by the alchemy of his genius."[149]

Finally, with a flourish of inconsistency affected by transcendentalists from Emerson to Whitman, sometimes consciously and more often unconsciously, and forgetful of the fact that he had, only a few minutes earlier, crowned Kant as the high-priest of "Free Religionists," "Unitarians," and "agnostics . . . and all that class," he concludes: ". . . here was a grand mind to whom we are all indebted; and we shall no longer go into that realm where went the deists and that class of people, and tried to solve the riddle of the world through their senses. Kant lifted us from that, and showed us that there is something in our minds not derived from the senses, that the senses can only reflect what is in the mind. What a step that was! to take us out of our senses and show us that they can only reflect in images the ideas in the mind; which are innate, eternal; that we brought them with us at birth as truth, justice, love, mercy, and beauty, being all revelations and intuitions."[150]

The comment about Kant's supplying "the step that was . . . to take us out of our senses" was, of course, an unintentional witticism that probably went unmarked; but we may be sure that if either Brokmeyer or Snider had been present, one or the other would have improved the occasion to indulge in a little word-play.

Here Mr. Cohn, one of the "students," ventured to "offer a criticism" of the Dean's interpretation, by emphasizing the difference between *Pure* and *Practical* Reason and by relating the word *practical* to its original meaning: "To do, to act, to make." "The great philosophical discovery of Kant," as Cohn saw it, is that "as long as we remain in the domain of pure thinking, our mind criticizing itself, we fatally come to utter skepticism. But we are in a world of action; we cannot withdraw from it. We *have* to act, and so truth is to be found not in the abstract simplicity of thinking, but in the concrete complexity of life, so that we must not go from philosophy to ethics, but from ethics to philosophy. That is why Kant comes to more definite conclusions in his 'Critique of Practical Reason' than in the 'Critique of Pure Reason,' although the conclusions at which he arrives may be criticized." Cohn was not too much concerned with how "definite" or indefinite Kant's conclusions were; he was not concerned at all about Kant's conclusions. What did interest him was Kant's "method." Accordingly he concluded on a note that could hardly have harmonized with Alcott's thinking: "The whole is a question of method."[151]

At this point Harris took the floor. Although he was not scheduled for this part of the program with a formal paper, what he delivered at the time has all the earmarks of having been prepared in advance. He began by taking up Alcott's analogical metaphor of Kant as the Columbus of speculation, but objected to the suggestion that Kant often "put out his sounding-lines and brought up nothing." After a passing reference of agreement to Jones' point that neither Kant nor any philosopher has yet said "the last word," he proceeded to a discussion of the paper read the day before by George Sylvester Morris, formerly a lecturer of philosophy at Johns Hopkins University, recently installed Professor of Philosophy at the University of Michigan, the translator of Ueberweg, and now working on a critical exposition of Kant's *Critique of Pure Reason* (published the next year).[152] The general tenor of his remarks was to emphasize the natural process of development and, at the same time, the essential unity of thought that runs from Plato and Aristotle, through Kant, Fichte, Schelling, and Schleiermacher, to Hegel. To find the "fundamental" and "central" principles of this essential unity that will give us "rational explanations and reduce the many to the one, and show that the many belong to a system," it is necessary to take into account all "previous philosophers." For "the finding of the one in the many is reducing the many to a system—not as with a rope of sand, but reducing the many to an organic whole through the discovery of dependence and essential relation."[153] As for the objection that philosophy employs a "technique" that is both "unnecessary" or "pedantic," what is needed, to find this "Primal Philosophy and Theology," is not a less technical terminology but a more precise and a more special one. A technique designed for "finite things" and fragments of the universe" will never prove adequate for the explanation of "infinitude" and "totality."[154] Although Harris usually had scant praise for eclecticism and eclectic methods of the sort he recommended on this occasion, his recommendation was doubtless made in view of the need he felt for greater harmony than the remarks thus far had engendered. And on this note of harmony the morning session of the Kant Centennial adjourned, as soon as Professor J. W. Mears had added his bit of justification of Kant: "The difficulty about . . . Kant has been, not, as Mrs. Howe has intimated, that he had 'too much theological baggage,' but that he had too much infidel baggage. We could not get people to study him, because they thought that he was the father and source of all the so-called rationalism of Germany. . . . [The] fact [is] that that sort of thing was there before Kant, but he gave it its death-blow."[155]

In the afternoon, President John Bascom of the University of Wisconsin read the principal paper, on "The Freedom of the Will, Empirically Considered," prefacing it "with some criticisms of Kant, and also some remarks upon philosophical technique," in which he contended that philosophic terminology should be translatable into common language. "If philosophy be ultimately a settling of the limits of authority of human knowledge, then it must take hold of human knowledge where it exists in the minds of the mass of men and explain it there, and apply all its limitations and principles there and not elsewhere."[156]

Immediately following Bascom's address, Samuel Emery arose to say, "while somebody else is getting ready to speak," that though he, too, had had some trouble with the Kantian time, space, and categories (if viewed as purely subjective), it might reasonably be doubted that Kant was being fairly interpreted by Dr. Bascom, who put a "subjective" construction upon them. With regard to Bascom's explanation of Kant on free-will and liberty, he agreed heartily.[157]

By the time Emery had finished, Harris was ready. In view of what he had said at the close of the morning session regarding the technique of philosophy, he interpreted President Bascom's criticism of philosophical terminology as being directed at him. This time he spoke extemporaneously. "I could not help thinking carefully [said Harris] as Professor Bascom was reading, about the point he made in regard to technical terms, and which I could not quite understand," because while Bascom had seemed, in his prefatory remarks, to disparage the use of special terms, he had gone on to use technically philosophical words "derived from a good many systems," and had given to them varying applications.[158] Far from disparaging technique in philosophical speculation, Harris repeated his argument for a more exact and perfect technique, at the same time calling upon President Bascom's "long experience in teaching philosophy" to bear out his contention that "The most fearful technique in philosophy is that of a person who uses a common term in a special sense and yet leaves the reader to think that he is using it in an ordinary sense."[159] Yes, Harris' mellifluous voice, too, concealed a stinger which he knew how to flash on occasions.

Then he went on to show how, if rightly understood, the seemingly special and "subjective" nomenclature of Kant could be brought into harmony with the more generally familiar "objective" terms of Aristotle.[160] For himself, he added, he "satisfied himself with the Greek basis," all the more because he saw Aristotle and Kant as coming "to the same result" as regards the bridging of "the chasm between subjective and objective."[161]

At this point Sanborn, evidently anxious to avoid a squally session, suggested that all might find a harmonious and common ground in Emerson, through whom more than "all other persons combined . . . the Kantian movement has affected America."[162] He went on to argue for catholicity, embracing (1) Kant, regarding whom, he said, we have heard "many things" throughout the week, (2) Fichte, "concerning whom we shall hear a paper next week by Mr. Edwin D. Mead," (3) Schelling and Schleiermacher, whose influence Emerson had done so much to spread through his reports in *The Dial,* supplied to him directly from Germany by Mr. Charles Stearns Wheeler and also by direct contact with J. Elliot Cabot, and (4) Hegel, of whom, "of course we have heard much."[163]

And Alcott, taking his cue from Sanborn, went on to deliver the valedictory upon the Kant Centennial by reminding all that "Human faculties are differently cast into different types." "It is in vain," he said, "for persons of a certain type to attempt, without very long effort and a probable failure, to look at things in a purely philosophical manner; and it is equally impossible, ordinarily, for those of another type to look at them in any other than a poetic manner . . . Do not seek to put your minds, those of you who are not logical, into logical forms, thinking that you must learn that alphabet to know anything; neither shall I say to you who are logical, put your thoughts into poetic forms . . . Goethe and Emerson and Shakespeare and Dante, and the great poets of the past, occupy a wide space in the world's history, and interest a large class of people in their manner. So do the great thinkers, Aristotle, Plato,

Kant, Hegel, Schelling, and Fichte. But do you not see that you could not put each one into the other's brains? It could not be done."[164]

Having delivered this "charge" to the scholars sitting before him, the Dean went on to pronounce the benediction in the following terms: "The beauty of this school is that we have those who speak from these different aspects, so that we gather an idea of the different modes in which thought works. We call it a School of Philosophy, it is true. Mr. Emerson puts his philosophy into warm tropes, and paints pictures with his words. But Hegel and that class of thinkers strip off the image and give you the pure, absolute truth as it lies in their minds. Mr. Emerson could not have had his influence in the world had he endeavored to do his work as Hegel did . . . Imagination and reason are the opposite poles of one sphere. The poet and the philosopher work differently, but they do the same work."[165] With this final word of wisdom the Concord Kant Centennial came to a triumphant and harmonious close.[166]

However often Alcott reminded his "Faculty" of the virtues of tolerance and of catholicity of taste, there remained an undercurrent of frictional rivalry between the Platonists and the Hegelians, the poets and the metaphysicians. Alcott himself had reflected, immediately upon the close of the second summer school, that "the purely intellectual aspects of philosophy, as systematized by foreign masters, particularly Plato and Hegel, have had an undue ascendancy, to the obscuring for the time, and suppression even of the spiritual and ideal," as he understood them.[167] It was therefore decided that the program for the fourth session (1882) should be arranged in such a way that the lines of methodology would be less sharply drawn. The leading lecturers were, as before, Harris, Jones, Alcott, Kedney, Sanborn, and Watson. Alcott was to go on, as before, to expound his own philosophy, in four lectures; but Harris' ten lectures were to be less strictly Hegelian and less abstruse than heretofore: five were to treat of the general history of philosophy, three of Fichte, and two of art; while Jones' eight lectures, instead of expounding Plato solely, were to deal, four of them, with Christian philosophy, three with Oriental thought, and only one with Plato. Still greater catholicity and breadth was sought by having Sanborn deliver three lectures on oracular philosophy; Watson, three on Kant, Schelling, and Fichte; and Kedney, four on the philosophy of aesthetics; while among the special lecturers who gave only one discourse at this session were presented Alexander Wilder of Newark, Jones' editor of the *Journal of the American Akademe,* who spoke on Alexandrian Platonism, Noah Porter on Kantian ethics, James McCosh on the Scottish philosophy, George H. Howison on German philosophy since Hegel, R. A. Holland on Atomism, C. A. Bartol on the Nature of Knowledge, and R. G. Hazard on the Utility of Metaphysical Pursuits.[168]

But Harris' lectures on the history of philosophy turned out to have a strongly Hegelian cast; those on Fichte presented Fichte in relation to Hegel; and his two discourses on art were pure Hegelian *Aes-thetik*. And Jones, whether he was down for a lecture on Christ, Maga, or the relation of science to philosophy, discoursed on Plato. Jones still remained one of the major attractions, but his position had grown progressively subordinate to that of Harris. Even Alcott found himself less and less drawn to the Jacksonville Platonist with his earnest but interminable Platonic expositions. Moreover, Harris had moved to Concord: his influence was more nearly present and compelling than that of Dr. Jones in far-away Illinois. Before the fourth school opened, Alcott wrote significantly in his *Journals,* "Sanborn and Harris are now taking warm and sweet places in my regard."[169] Thus Hegel came gradually to get the better of Plato, until, by the end of the 1882-session, it was apparent to the Jacksonville contingent that unless the Concord "ring" of Hegelians could be broken up, Jones would not be able to maintain a position of respectable and coordinate leadership with Harris. Snider professed to have seen this inevitable conclusion to the rivalry as early at least as 1881,[170] but then Snider's second-sight was often better than his fore-sight. The Westerners from Illinois, Missouri, and Indiana therefore got together to hold a caucus, whence they emerged with the decision, since so many of the students were from the Midwest, to ask that the next year the School be held there, and that thereafter it should alternate between the East and the West.

When the decision went against the Western petitioners, they were keenly disappointed, none more than Dr. Jones. Some of them, notably the St. Louisans, remained faithful to Concord and continued to attend; but others, especially those from Illinois, ceased going and joined efforts with Jones in the formation, the next year, of the American Akademe in Jacksonville. Jones maintained cordial personal relations with Alcott, Sanborn, Emery, Harris, and others of the Concord School, but he never again appeared on any of its programs or attended any of its meetings, thus making inevitable the eclipse of Plato by Hegel in Concord. Henceforth the Platonic tradition centering around Jones and incorporated in the American Akademe as a winter school was felt to be an antidote and in some sense a rival of the Hegelian school at Concord, which continued as a summer school.

The withdrawal had other important effects beyond the triumph of Hegel over Plato in Concord.

The departure of Jones and his colleagues meant not only the loss of a number of hitherto faithful attendants but also the loss of adequate competition and consequently a diminution in the intensity of philosophical discussion, thus preparing the way for the encroachment of the literary upon the more purely philosophical interests of the School.

This last trend did not become immediately apparent. The program for 1883 included the usual course of lectures by Harris on Hegel and the philosophy of the absolute; Howison lectured on Hume and Kant; and Sanborn on Puritanic philosophy, Franklin, and Emerson. The most distinctive feature was William James' three lectures on Psychology.[171] But, as regards the general tendency of development in future years, the most noteworthy element of the 1883-school was the recall of Snider (absent during the preceding session, for he had become a bit obstreperous and not too mindful of the Concord reticences) to present an exegesis in four lectures of the second of his "Literary Bibles," namely, Homer. This literary tendency was further accentuated in lectures by Miss E. P. Peabody on "Milton's *Paradise Lost*," John Albee on "The Norman Influence in English Language and Literature," Edwin D. Mead on "Carlyle and Emerson," Mrs. Julia W. Howe on "Margaret Fuller," Julian Hawthorne on "The Novel," Mrs. Cheney on "Hindu Literature," Dr. Kedney on

"Art Appreciation" and on "The Higher Criticism," and Blake's reading from Thoreau's Manuscripts.[172]

Snider considered the third session, that of 1881 (the second in which he participated), "the culmination of the School" and "its best and happiest year," because in later years he missed "the same up-spring ... the same spontaneous overflow of enthusiasm."[173] What he refers to is that in 1881 "the two main threads of the School" were then most harmoniously "spun alongside of each other by those two ardent philosophic spinners, Dr. Harris and Dr. Jones, propagandists of Hegel and Plato, respectively."[174] Even then he "often heard the whispered decision: 'Dr. Harris has taken intellectual possession of the School' ... It was the general consensus of the best of those present."[175] As we have seen, Dr. Jones retired the next year, taking with him a clientele that was sorely missed. But all the indications are that the "best" year, the climax, came about 1883. Emerson died in 1882, and he had always been a powerful magnet drawing many people to the Concord School if only to see him, even though he never took a very active part in the School itself. The program for 1884 (the sixth) was devoted almost exclusively to Emerson.[176] It marked a period in Emerson's influence; henceforth his personal influence, particularly as far as the Concord School was concerned, steadily diminished. Alcott's health grew progressively worse.

Most important by way of changing the character of the School, destroying first its distinctively philosophical character and contributing ultimately to the death of the School itself, was the increasingly literary character which it assumed. The session of 1883 already had been deflected largely from its philosophical course; that of 1884 was devoted almost solely to Emerson, with considerable emphasis upon his literary character; the program for 1885 was dedicated to Goethe almost entirely, nineteen of the lectures being devoted to Goethe, while five speakers contributed to "A Symposium: Is Pantheism the Legitimate Outcome of Modern Science?"[177]

The lectures on Goethe at the seventh Concord School (1885) represent a landmark in the history of Goethe's vogue and influence in the United States, and they provide an illuminating commentary on the state of American literary culture as represented by the particular climate of culture typified by the Concord idealists.[178] But they suggest also that the tradition of speculative thought in America was not yet strong enough to avoid being dissipated, for they indicate that a marked change had taken place in the School to deflect it from the original "aim of the Faculty . . . to bring together a few of those persons who, in America, have pursued, or desire to pursue, the paths of speculative philosophy; to encourage these students and professors to communicate with each other what they have learned and meditated; and to illustrate, by a constant reference to poetry and higher literature, those ideas which philosophy presents."[179] Another change is suggested by the fact that the directors could no longer count upon the same singleness of purpose, unanimity of interest, and general knowledge of their students, all of which they had taken for granted during the earlier years; for in 1885 they began to distribute in advance bibliographies and lists of readings for the better preparation of the students for the lectures and to encourage their more general participation in the discussions.[180]

Estimates vary regarding the preparation of the students who came to Concord from 1879 to 1887. Denton Snider always spoke a little disdainfully of the intelligence of his hearers at Concord. By his own account, he sometimes could not resist giving way to the imp of the perverse and spilling over into some *diablerie* at the expense of the Concordians, in a manner to shock or offend the gentry of "vacant face-long gravity" who sat before him.[181] He sometimes doubted that the "smiling appreciation" with which they listened to lectures was always synonymous with "adequate understanding," and himself related with obvious satisfaction the story current that the erudite lectures could be tersely summed up as "What's mind? Never matter. What's matter?

Never mind," as well as the report that the Concord Faculty was much concerned with "the Whatness of the Howsoever" and "the Thingness of the Why." While he hastened to add, "I never heard such talk there,"[182] Snider often displayed an ugly disposition when he compared the Concord school with his own in St. Louis, Milwaukee, Cincinnati, Chicago, and elsewhere,[183] when he repeated with gusto bits of gossip overhead in the Concord barber shop regarding the Hillside Philosophers,[184] and when he did not neglect to repeat the quip of a Concord wiseacre who spoke of Sleepy Hollow as being Concord's "chief civic asset."[185] Charitable and benign as Snider could be, he could seldom forego the temptation to belittle and sometimes to indulge his desire to take sharp tweaks in the sides of those who most befriended him, particularly in situations where he had to yield to them the leadership. At the Concord School of Philosophy, he maintained, "the chief shortcoming . . . sprang from the lack of previous preparation of its students and listeners." "I felt certain that half of the audience during the Concord Goethe School had never read *Faust,* or at most only in a very desultory way. Indeed, when I lectured on Shakespeare, using some of the incidents of *Love's Labor Lost* for my purpose, I found reason to believe that not one in four of my hearers had ever grappled with that somewhat difficult and less known play. And when Harris talked his unmixed Hegel to that mixed crowd, though he tried to popularize his ponderous nomenclature, and did to a certain extent, I could see by the corrugated foreheads and tensely shutting eyelids, that quite everybody there needed some preliminary training to the hard language and to the still harder thought."[186]

Here, again, one cannot be sure that Snider is quite fair to the Concordians. In his own "Literary Schools" and "Communal Universities," where he held the undisputed leadership, he took care, of course, to educate his pupils during the off-season in smaller classes, which served, at the same time, also as recruiting stations for the larger annual schools. Consequently the Western schools were, in Snider's estimation, what the Eastern schools should have been.

That there were many who went to Concord for no more serious purposes than those which inspire Chautauqua-addicts and institute-goers is obvious; but it seems equally clear, from the stature of many of the lecturers and the excellence of their lectures, that the intellectual fare offered at Concord was phenomenally good, and that many who partook of it necessarily profited by it. Men of the caliber of Harris, Howison, Morris, Fiske, James, Royce, Porter, and Bascom would hardly have devoted their time and energies to sham philosophical and literary feasts.

The fact remains, however, that about 1886 the course of the Concord School of Philosophy went rapidly downward. The inadequacy of its "scholars" cannot have been the only cause. The "Faculty" remained, to the end, as distinguished as they had been during the earlier years, though some of them were beginning to develop tangential interests. Harris, for example, was turning more and more toward practical educational matters and was soon to go to Washington as Commissioner of Education. Emery returned to the West, and Alcott died in 1888. Some responsibility for the decline of the School must be attributed to the loss, beginning in 1883, of its distinctively speculative character. Following the Emerson School of 1884 and the Goethe School of 1885, the two weeks of the 1886-School were divided equally between Dante and Plato;[187] and while for the ninth and last session, that of 1887, the directors returned to their original aim of pursuing "the paths of speculative philosophy" by devoting the major part of the program to Aristotle,[188] even to publishing in advance, in the *Journal of Speculative Philosophy,* an elaborate bibliography and "Hints to Students,"[189] Alcott's Concord "university" came to an end almost simultaneously with his own earthly existence.

Two general observations appear to be in order. First, we may observe that American Transcendentalism, originating in the vicinity of Boston, had there its first notable efflorescence during the thirties and forties. Thence it migrated westward, or was carried thither—by lectures, essays, reviews, books, by young ministers, editors, and particularly by New England pedagogues, who spread their sphere of influence fanwise over the West and Northwest— where it did its most fruitful and practical work in a pioneer state of society, even while it became decentralized into groups, circles, and cults that exercised their own individuality to such degrees as to make their common origin hardly preceptible. The movements in Missouri and Illinois, wherever else they derived their nourishment, drew heavily upon New England Transcendentalism; and though freelances like Snider and Jones believed their destiny lay in the West and therefore desired to declare their independence from Plymouth Rock, and others like Davidson denied allegiance to anybody or anything, all of them eventually gravitated toward the East. In the name of Alcott and under the direction of Harris, American idealism returned to its original fountain-head. Finally, through the instrumentality of efficient propagandists like Harris, it was given a wider and more practical application, notably in the

one hundred eleven

educational system (elementary, secondary, and collegiate) of the United States.

In the second place, it is to be noted that in Germany, transcendentalism developed progressively from Kant, through men like Fichte, Schelling, and Schleiermacher, to reach its culmination in Hegel. From Kantian epistemological and ontological techniques, it developed a tendency to find applications in socialized religious forms by Schleiermacher and in ethico-political forms by Fichte, to receive its final institutionalization in Hegel. In America, if some allowance is made for natural differences, a similar, though by no means identical, progression is discernable. American Transcendentalism, in Emerson's hands, originated a theory under the impetus of a Kantian terminology, however widely Kant and Emerson diverged at other points. In the hands of men like Ripley, Transcendentalism took on elements of Fichtean ethics and assimilated something of the socialization of religion as taught by Schleiermacher and Ronge; while in the West, Brokmeyer, Harris and their colleagues, in their pursuit and practice of Hegelian principles, represented in some respects the anti-thetical movement. Finally, using Alcott, Jones, and Harris as the media, all differences and opposites were drawn together and given something like a synchronization or synthesis in Concord. Hegelians like Snider and Harris could not fail to observe that the course of American idealism during the nineteenth century, as affected by German absolutism, was but another illustration of the Hegelian triadic dialectic of thesis, antithesis, and synthesis.

VII. Abiding Effects

Undoubtedly the greatest single and most lasting effect of the St. Louis Movement as it can be traced today, instead of being strictly within the realm of philosophy, is to be recognized in the work that Harris performed as Commissioner of Education in channelizing, systematizing, and standardizing the public school system of the United States on Hegelian lines. The fixed and absolute principles upon which he proceeded in his organization, correlation, and conservation of educational forces and resources were destined, during the twentieth century, to be modified by the onslaught of the New Education that became articulate even while he was still in complete command. The revolt begun in 1894 by B. A. Hinsdale, and carried forward the next year by Charles DeGarmo and the two McMurrays, set up in opposition to the dogma of formal discipline and Hegelian principles of psychology and educational organization a body of ideas drawn chiefly from Herbart and Rein of Jena. Then came the day when G. Stanley Hall, with his brilliant platform method, preached eloquently the gospel of a wholly different psychology from that taught by Harris; and eventually the forces of James, Dewey, *et al* overwhelmed Hegelian absolutism in American education, leaving only a few die-hards to sing the praises of Harris, the Great Conservator,[190] to proclaim him "the one truly great philosophical mind which has yet appeared on the western continent,"[191] and to assert, all appearances to the contrary, that the spirit of Hegel and Harris still marches on. It may be remarked, despite the manifestly sweeping changes that have come over the spirit of American elementary education, that the late President Nicholas Murray Butler was essentially correct when he observed in 1929 that Harris' work was so well done as to be "already almost forgotten."[192] That is to say, the American public school system is so much the development of Harris' principles and the result of his labors that the product, especially in its fundamental organizational aspects, is indistinguishable from the principles that motivated and shaped it.

In most other respects, however, the influence of the St. Louis Movement becomes elusive and evanescent when we try to appraise it in terms of the twentieth century. While Harris' multiform activities, Snider's widespread operations, Brokmeyer's great personal magnetism, Davidson's flittings hither and thither, and the great bulk of their published words, all insinuated themselves in some degree into the life and sum-total of American culture and became a part of it, the movement as such dissipated itself without leaving many clearly recognizable tokens. The latest survivor was the Denton J. Snider Association for Universal Culture with headquarters in St. Louis, which persevered in its study programs until 1930 and annually made a visit to Snider's grave until the depressed thirties sent it on the way that many such anachronistic relics went during that discouraging decade.

It may be that if Harris had adopted a more popular tone and terminology for the twenty-two volumes of the *Journal of Speculative Philosophy,* he might have won a larger hearing among nineteenth-century Americans for his philosophy which offered so many conciliations in an age that was a compound of contradictions and oppositions. But that was not the way of William Torrey Harris. Convinced by Brokmeyer that the only proper explanation of history lay in the Hegelian law of dialectical growth, he chose to move in the rarified atmosphere of scholastic symbols, even to the point of subordinating Hegel's ethical and political works to the sixth and seventh places in a list of eight, in which the *Logic* is placed first.[193] The wonder is that, in his educational endeavors, he succeeded as well as he did in giving currency and cogency to his abstruse phrases and his fine-spun doctrines among the teachers and public-school administrators of his day. What's more, if he had addressed himself more largely to the popular audience, he would surely have missed winning the academic allies who, as things turned out, provided the chief stronghold in which his type of thinking was fostered and perpetuated.

It may be that the St. Louisans would have been more successful in perpetuating their philosophy if they had stuck more closely to the profession which bred them in the first place. The great majority of them started in the high schools of St. Louis. Although most of them remained teachers in some sense of the word, they did not continue to work within the common framework of teaching in the organized schools; and few of the original group were ambitious to take regularly appointed academic positions in established colleges and universities. Only George H. Howison, the first vice president of the Philosophical Society, was a regular academician. In 1871 he left Washington University, and after holding various collegiate appointments and studying at the University of Berlin, went in 1884 to the University of California, where he remained as a professor until his death in 1916. He wrote extensively, raised Berkeley to a western center for philosophical studies, and drew a great number of brilliant young men into the scope of his influence—some of them, like Professor Arthur O. Lovejoy, active today. During his St. Louis period he participated in the deliberations of the Philosophical Society; in 1883 he contributed an extended essay on German philosophy to the *Journal*; and he took part in the fifth (1883) and the seventh (1885) sessions of the Concord School of Philosophy. But eventually he demonstrated his individualism and originality by becoming virtually the founder of personalism. Something of the original Hegelian impulse was unquestionably imparted to the successive generations of his students, but he veered further and further away from the absolute idealism of Hegel in favor of a form of personal idealism or spiritual pluralism. Thus the great following which he built up became as much a dissipating as a perpetuating force, so far as the St. Louis Movement was concerned.[194]

One other who was more or less closely identified with various individuals of the St. Louis group, notably Harris, was George Sylvester Morris, though his enthusiasm for Kant and Hegel was acquired independently of the St. Louisans. He wrote for the *Journal of Speculative Philosophy.* As a professor at Johns Hopkins University and the University of Michigan he became widely known as a champion of Hegel and Kant and as a co-worker with Harris in the publication of the "Griggs Philosophical Series" of German Philosophy, which he edited, and in which he himself published *Kant's Critique of*

Pure Reason, a Critical Exposition (1882) and
Hegel's Philosophy of the State and of History
(1887).[195] His translation of Ueberweg's *History
of Philosophy* in 1873 marks an important epoch in
the history of the study of philosophy in America.
Morris' influence is another example of the type of
following and influence which the St. Louis Hegelians might have secured for themselves if, instead of
expending their energies on semi-popular groups,
communal universities, summer schools, and philosophical clubs of various complexions, they had
sought the stability and permanence of regular academic appointments. Certainly Harris and Kroeger,
possibly Snider, and undoubtedly others of the long
list of writers for the *Journal of Speculative Philosophy* possessed, or could readily have acquired, the
requisite qualifications.

Looking back upon the eighties and nineties as
we can today, we have no difficulty seeing that while
the media through which the St. Louisans chose to
work tended in the end to diffuse or dilute rather
than to prolong and preserve the ideals for which
they strove, Hegel in more academic accoutrements
nevertheless conquered many of the philosophy de-
partments in American colleges and universities, and
often those of history and political science as well.
The conquest was, in some instances, short-lived; but
while it lasted, it was pretty general. But the Hegel-

ization of our universities was more the result of the trek of American students to the German universities and of the influences of English and Continental intermediaries than of direct connections with the semi-popular Hegelian movement on native soil. Royce, for example, learned his absolute idealism in Germany, where he studied with Lotze, Wundt, and Windelband of Göttingen and Leipzig. Peirce turned directly to Kant's Critiques; as for Hegel, whose philosophy he said "mine resuscitates, though in a strange dress,"[196] he got something from Morris at Hopkins but more from Augusto Vera's commentaries in the *Journal of Speculative Philosophy* and still more from Hegel's books themselves. Palmer acquired his knowledge of German idealism partly in Germany and (particularly as it affects Hegel) from the books of the Scotch Hegelians Stirling and Caird, as well as from Hegel's works. James studied in Germany, read the Germans themselves, and consulted their commentators. Hall, Ladd, Cattell, Baldwin, and Münsterberg imported experimental psychology directly from Germany. There were exceptions, to be sure. Howison and Morris have already been cited as examples. Among Harris' contributors to his *Journal* were Benjamin Rand, G. Stanley Hall, Josiah Royce, Charles S. Peirce, William James, and John Dewey, all of whom became philosophers in their own right and professors of philosophy in American universities. To most of these the Hegelian *Journal* was more than an outlet for their first efforts at philosophical writing, and all of them acknowledged that German philosophy exerted a shaping influence in the development of their own philosophical personality; but the greater impetus directing them to a consideration of German thought came from quarters other than St. Louis. William James, for example, even while grudgingly acknowledging that Hegel's influence on him "remained always more or less pronounced,"[197] usually poked good-natured fun at the St. Louis Hegelians.[198] On the other hand, John Dewey, whose primary sources of inspiration were obviously not St. Louis, and whose final position developed much beyond anything he could have learned from Hegel, nevertheless wrote to Harris on December 17, 1886: "When I was studying the German philosophers I read something of yours on them of which one sentence has always remained with me . . . you spoke of the 'great psychological movement from Kant to Hegel' . . . one thing I have attempted to do is to translate a part at least of the significance of that movement into our present psychological movement."[199] So it is that only occasional glimpses and indications remain of close cause-and-effect relationships between the academicians and the men of St. Louis.

There was no dearth of personal contacts between

them. Even in Tom Davidson's quixotic retreat, Josiah Royce, William James, and John Dewey found themselves eating at the same table with the men from Jacksonville, Osceola, St. Louis, and Concord. But the point is that little came of these contacts. They turned out to be tangential and peripheral. The case of the philosophers' retreat at Glenmore is symbolic. Tom Davidson's death in 1900 cut short his elaborate plans to insure perpetuity to his "beautiful Academe." It had been Davidson's design to make his Glenmore school the culmination of all the philosophical ferments that had gone before, just as it was the hope of the St. Louisans to effect the consummation of American idealism, first, through the instrumentality of the Philosophical Society and, later, through the Literary School and the Communal University. Alcott and his allies had similar plans for the Concord School. In the end, all were swept aside by the times. The naturalistic trend of a new age made headway, however resolutely Jones opposed it at Jacksonville or Alcott in Concord. It was no mere coincidence that the Plato Club, the American Akademe, the Philosophical Society, the Concord School of Philosophy, the *Journal of the American Akademe,* the *Bibliotheca Platonica,* and the *Journal of Speculative Philosophy* all came to an end within the short period of five years (1887-1892). The same five years saw the first appearance of *The Monist*

(1890-1936), the *International Journal of Ethics* (1890———), and the *Philosophical Review* (1892-———), which, together with the *Journal of Philosophy* (1904———), remained until recently the chief periodicals for the publication and exchange of philosophical opinion in the United States. The Western Philosophical Association was established in 1900, and the American Philosophical Association in 1901. All announced in unmistakable terms that a new era had begun, that the old dispensation, however much the new might be indebted to the old, was dead. In the search for a distinctively "American" philosophy, there were few who agreed with Walt Whitman that "Only Hegel is fit for America—is large enough and free enough . . . an essential and crowning justification of New World democracy."[200]

Struggling as they did against hopeless odds, the half-dozen idealistic schools and movements—East and West—put up a stiff resistence from 1836 to the end of the century against what came increasingly to be called "the American philosophy." Time and again, especially after 1880, the idealists were forced to retreat. In every counter-offensive that they launched, they marched under the banner of Kant, or Hegel, or Plato—or all three. But their best efforts at union were ineffectual. After the cycle from Concord to St. Louis, to Jacksonville, and back to Concord was once completed, it was not repeated, first because the times were against absolute idealism of whatever kind, and second, because the nineteenth-century idealists had neglected to train among the younger generation able successors to take over and to carry forward the movements which had, in all instances, depended too exclusively upon individual leadership. The individualism of "self-activity" developed no less in New England Transcendentalism than in St. Louis Hegelianism failed to breed the necessary community of interest and solidity of association to perpetuate either of them as a movement or as an institution.

However, while failing radically to change or even to deflect the direction of American thought, the several groups, taking them altogether, did assist significantly in the revitalization of the oft-dormant and equally oft-recurrent strain of idealism that has been a vital part of American consciousness from earliest Puritan days, and that, thanks to the nineteenth-century idealists, still runs deeply through the American mind. This they effected because they never surrendered or admitted themselves utterly defeated, even while they bowed before the more strongly organized forces of naturalism and materialism.

Another important service which they performed was that in their insistence upon free inquiry, even when it threatened traditionalism, they proved strong allies and supporters of the long line of liberal

American academicians from James Marsh of Vermont and Henry Boynton Smith of Amherst to Josiah Royce at Harvard and J. E. Creighton of Cornell[201] who fought a slow but increasingly successful fight to liberate American philosophy from a too-exclusive domination by Lockean sensationalism on the one hand and by Scottish common-sense on the other. Emerson and Jones, Harris and Emery, no less than this succession of professors of philosophy, opposed academic tradition and professional prejudices: (1) the deep-seated prejudice in American universities in favor of the entire Lockean tradition, and (2) the prevalent prejudice against any brand of philosophy that emanated from Germany, whether critical or romantic. In these aims, however widely they differed in other particulars, the Platonic intuitionalists of Concord and Jacksonville and the Hegelian rationalists of Quincy and St. Louis were united no less among themselves than with the professors of philosophy and of theology who were beginning to develop a sense of historicity and of criticism. Thus they helped prepare the way for twentieth-century freedom and objectivity that permitted the evolution of the pragmatic, or the "American" philosophy, which they opposed, and which, as things turned out, spelled the doom of their hope that idealism might become the prevailing American philosophy.

But while late-nineteenth and early twentieth-century winds of new doctrine swept all these early semi-popular philosophical currents before them, the academic halls remained places where the tradition of idealism from Kant to Hegel could find a domicile promising security and a degree of perpetuity. The significant shaping influences of German philosophy upon the idealism of Royce, the psychology of Münsterberg, the pragmatism of Peirce and James, and the educational philosophy of Dewey are later and transmuted manifestations of a long process of acculturation that earlier conditioned New England Transcendentalism, that was carried forward by the St. Louisans and the Concordians, and that persists very markedly in current pragmatism, as well as in the current academic tradition of philosophical instruction in American colleges and universities. By such means and avenues, the several motifs of German philosophical idealism have become so deeply imbedded in the course of constructive thought in America that the termination of its influence cannot be envisaged unless American thinking itself should come to an end.

Notes and References

[1] The chief sources of information on Brokmeyer's life, as well as on the St. Louis Movement, are Brokmeyer's journal, *A Mechanic's Diary*, ed. by Eugene C. Brokmeyer, Washington, D. C., 1910; Denton J. Snider's autobiography, *A Writer of Books in His Genesis*, St. Louis, 1910, and his history of *The St. Louis Movement in Philosophy, Literature, Education, Psychology, with Chapters of Autobiography*, St. Louis, 1920; Charles M. Perry, *The St. Louis Movement in Philosophy: Some Source Material*, Norman, Okla., 1930; D. H. Harris (ed.), *A Brief Report on the Meeting Commemorative of the Early Saint Louis Movement . . . in Honor of Dr. Denton J. Snider's Eightieth Birthday Held January 14th and 15th 1921 . . .* Los Angeles, 1921; Cleon Forbes, "The St. Louis School of Thought," *Missouri Historical Review* XXV, i (Oct., 1930), 83-101; ii (Jan., 1931), 289-305; iii (April, 1931), 461-473; iv (July, 1931), 609-623; XXVI, i (Oct., 1931), 68-77; William Schuyler, "German Philosophy in St. Louis," *Bulletin of the Washington University Association*, no. 2, April 23, 1904 (St. Louis, 1904), 62-89; and information supplied by Brokmeyer's son, Mr. Eugene C. Brokmeyer of Washington, D. C.

[2] See the essays by William Torrey Harris, "How I Was Educated," *Forum*, I (Aug., 1886), 552-561, and "Books That Have Helped Me," *Forum*, III (April, 1887), 142-151. Among the more comprehensive studies of Harris consulted, besides the bibliography in Charles M. Perry, *op. cit.*, 79-140, are the following: John S. Roberts, *William Torrey Harris: A Critical Study of His Educational and Related Philosophical Views*, Washington, D. C., 1924; Edward L. Schaub (ed.), *William Torrey Harris (1835-1935); A Collection of Essays . . . in Commemoration of Dr. Harris' Centennial . . .* Chicago and London, 1936; and the illuminating chapter on Harris in Professor Merle Curti's *Social Ideas of American Educators* (New York, 1935), 310-347. A biographical study, drawing upon the rich manuscript materials preserved by Miss Edith Davidson Harris, daughter of William Torrey Harris, at Walpole, N. H., has been prepared by Professor Kurt F. Leidecker of Troy, N. Y.

[3] Snider, *A Writer of Books*, 303.

[4] Cleon Forbes, *loc. cit.*, 91.

[5] Snider, *A Writer of Books,* 387-389; Johann G. Woerner, *The Rebel's Daughter: A Story of Love, Politics, and War* (Boston, 1899), 500-501.

[6] Snider, *St. Louis Movement,* 27; see also 28-29.

[7] Edward L. Schaub (ed.), *William Torrey Harris,* 30.

[8] Even while acknowledging his debt to New England Transcendentalism, Brokmeyer counselled his associates, "We must rise . . . above Parker, Alcott, and Emerson." Asked how that was to be accomplished, he had ready the answer, "By following the precepts of Kant's criticism, Hegel's speculative logic, and Goethe's humanism as exemplified in *Faust,* which is the greatest literary embodiment of both and the greatest poem of all time."—Snider, *A Writer of Books,* 391.

[9] Snider, *St. Louis Movement,* 52-59.

[10] *Ibid.,* 141.

[11] *Ibid.,* 142-143.

[12] Snider, *A Writer of Books,* 311-312.

[13] Kroeger and Woerner, the only other foreign-born among the earlier members, are not properly to be rated as leaders in the movement. Moreover, Kroeger came to America as a lad of eleven, and Woerner, at the age of seven.

[14] Snider, *St. Louis Movement,* 77. There developed a kind of craze that reached a crest in two series of publications: one beginning in 1869 with a twelve-page *Pamphlet for the People* (St. Louis, 1869), by Logan Uriah Reavis (the "Prophet of the Great Illusion"), which ran through numerous enlarged editions and culminated in his *A Change of National Empire; or, Arguments in Favor of the Removal of the National Capital from Washington City to the Mississippi Valley* (St. Louis, 1869, 170 pp.) ; and the other, Reavis' *Saint Louis: The Future Great City of the World,* which ran, in six years, through five editions—the first, in 1870, a modest booklet of 170 pages, and the last, the well-known Biographical Edition of 1875, a tome of 833 pages, plus 36 pages of introduction and 72 pages of appendices.

[15] In his autobiography Brokmeyer wrote what he preached daily to his disciples: "With self-determination as the ultimate principle of the universe, thought arrives at totality, and therefore at true objective internality, and not merely the subjective internality that predicates concerning an external. Thought is what is—the perennial, the external, and every determination thereof embodies or prefigures this, its nature. It is the internal for which the external is evanescent. It plays with form, for it itself is the substance, and the one substance in and of all forms."—*A Mechanic's Diary*, 24.

[16] An idea of the great variety of their literary endeavors can be gained readily by consulting the bibliographies in Charles M. Perry, *The St. Louis Movement in Philosophy: Some Source Material*, especially 84-96. Harris' writings, aggregating nearly five hundred titles, are listed separately, *ibid.*, 96-140.

[17] This is Harris' mature judgment, set down in 1890, in the preface to his work on *Hegel's Logic* (Chicago, 1890), xii.

[18] Snider, *St. Louis Movement*, 119; see also 204-205.

[19] *Ibid.*, 100.

[20] Quoted from a letter from Mr. E. C. Brokmeyer to the writer. See also the *Dictionary of American Biography* and Snider, *St. Louis Movement*, 100-102.

[21] See A. C. McGiffert, *Protestant Thought before Kant* (New York, 1911), 253.

[22] *The Letters of Ralph Waldo Emerson*, ed. by Ralph L. Rusk (6 vols., New York, 1939), V, 514.

[23] See Edward L. Schaub (ed.), *op. cit.*, 21-22.

[24] *Ibid.*, 70-71. See also Harvey G. Townsend, *Philosophical Ideas in the United States* (New York, 1934), chap. VIII, and Woodbridge Riley, *American Thought* (New York, 1915), 240-241, 248.

[25] Snider, *St. Louis Movement*, 190-192.

[26] For a discussion of the St. Louisans' philosophy of the family, economic society, the state, religion, and education, see Frances B. Harmon, *The Social Philosophy of the St. Louis Hegelians*, New York, 1943.

[27] Harris, *Hegel's Logic,* xii; see also Snider, *A Writer of Books,* 311-314.

[28] See F. B. Sanborn and W. T. Harris, *A. Bronson Alcott. His Life and Philosophy* (2 vols., Boston, 1893), II, 553; *Journals of Bronson Alcott,* ed. by Odell Shepard (Boston, 1938), 312-313.

[29] *A Mechanic's Diary* (Nov. 1, 1856), 229 *et seq.*

The discrepancy in the dates of Alcott's first visit as given by Brokmeyer (1856) and by his biographers (1858-1859) is explained in a letter (Dec. 30, 1940) to me from Brokmeyer's son, Mr. E. C. Brokmeyer (who edited his father's diary) in the following terms: "As the dates in father's 'Mechanic's Diary,' no attempt was made by me, or father, either, to make them correct; father had no patience with details and I confess to the same feeling. The dates are only approximate and perhaps based on recollection, poor at that."

While Brokmeyer was about the business of advancing the life of pure thought, he utterly disdained to quibble over details, even where his own name was involved. His works were published under the name of Brokmeyer (without the *c*), but on occasion he spelled it Brockmeyer; Harris, as well as Snider, generally wrote Brockmeyer, while Alcott used both interchangeably. To his son Engene, Brokmeyer often professed dissatisfaction with the English language as being entirely inadequate for reproducing the thought of Hegel. This impatience with language and other known traits of his character offer clues why, when Lewis J. Block undertook to revise and edit Brokmeyer's translation of Hegel's *Logic,* he found the task "too much for him." "The professor of philosophy" to whom the manuscript was next entrusted for editing professed it to be "too profound for him." (Charles M. Perry, *op. cit.,* 48-50.) However that may have been, some of the difficulty may be owing to traits of Brokmeyer mentioned (1) by William F. Woerner, who remarked, "Brokmeyer was the worst speller I have ever known and absolutely indifferent to grammatical construction," and (2) by Snider, who, while agreeing with Harris that in his talk Brokmeyer "barbed his weighty philosophy with flashes of lightning," had to admit that as a writer he was far less effective: "the cream of his genius . . . got quite skimmed off when he squeezed it through his pen-point into ink." (Snider, *St. Louis Movement*, 204-205, 207-208; see also *A Writer of Books*, 324-325.) It is worth noting that Brokmeyer was aware of his difficulties in rendering German into English. In *A Mechanic's Diary* (216) he tells the anecdote that when he brought a translation to his betrothed, for whose special benefit he had made it, she wanted to know, "Henry, what language did you translate that book into? You know I only speak English."

[80] *Journals of Alcott*, 378.

[81] Sanborn and Harris, *A. Bronson Alcott*, II, 553.

[82] *Journals of Alcott*, 379.

[83] *Ibid.*, 379.

[84] Sanborn and Harris, *A. Bronson Alcott*, II, 553.

[85] *Journals of Alcott*, 379.

[86] Compare *A Mechanic's Diary*, 229-231.

[87] *Journals of Alcott*, 279-280.

[88] *Ibid.*, 380.

[89] *Ibid.*, 380.

[40] *Ibid.*, 381.

[41] Snider, *A Writer of Books*, 335; see also Snider's *Biography of Ralph Waldo Emerson* (St. Louis, 1921), 257, 246-248.

[42] Snider, *A Writer of Books*, 335-336.

[43] *Ibid.*, 336.

[44] *Ibid.*, 337.

[45] *Journals of Alcott*, 381.

[46] Snider, *St. Louis Movement*, 268.

[47] *Ibid.*, 268.

[48] *Ibid.*, 268-269, 284-285, *et seq;* see also Snider, *A Writer of Books*, 431.

[49] Snider, *St. Louis Movement*, 307-308, 354-355.

[50] *Ibid.*, 267-268, 281-289, especially 285-286, 350-354. See also Austin Warren, "The Concord School of Philosophy," *New England Quarterly,* II, ii (April, 1929), 205.

[51] *Ibid.*, 270-271, 273-277, 285-286, 308.

[52] *Ibid.*, 326-338, 356-361.

[53] *Ibid.*, 359-361.

[54] Snider, *A Writer of Books,* 431.

[55] Snider, *St. Louis Movement,* 445.

[56] *Ibid.*, 269.

[57] Snider, *A Writer of Books,* 340.

[58] *Ibid.*, 341.

[59] *Ibid.*, 341-342.

[60] George F. Hoar, *Autobiography of Seventy Years* (2 vols., New York, 1903), I, 74.

[61] Odell Shepard, *Pedlar's Progress. The Life of Bronson Alcott* (Boston, 1937), 476, 481.

[62] *Journals of Bronson Alcott,* 382.

[63] *Ibid.*, 382.

[64] *Ibid.*, 383.

[65] *Ibid.*, 410-411; see also 419.

[66] Illustrative passages are to be found in the *Journals of Alcott,* 382, 383, 386, 388, 390, 399, 404, 408, 420, 423, 424-425, 428, 442, 444, 453-454, 486, 497, 499-500, 525, 536-537.

[67] *Ibid.*, 420.

[68] *Ibid.*, 424.

[69] *Ibid.*, 423.

[70] *Ibid.*, 444.

[71] *Ibid.*, 428.

[72] *Index,* XIII (Aug. 18, 1881), 78-79.

[73] Snider, *St. Louis Movement,* 282, 424, 427-429.

[74] *Letters of Emerson,* V, 421-422, 456, 500, 508; Sanborn and Harris, *A. Bronson Alcott,* II, 593; *Journals of Alcott,* 373.

[75] *Journals of Ralph Waldo Emerson* (10 vols., Boston and New York, 1909-1914), X, 130, 143-144.

[76] *Letters of Emerson,* IV, 530-531.

[77] *Ibid.,* V, 500, 508.

[78] Snider, *A Writer of Books,* 329.

[79] *Ibid.,* 329-330.

[80] *Ibid.,* 330.

[81] *Ibid,* 331.

[82] *Ibid.,* 331-332.

[83] The stages of Emerson's philosophical development, in its four epistemological phases, I shall treat in detail in my forthcoming study of German philosophical, educational, and literary influences in America.

[84] Snider, for his part, is rather voluble in his accounts of his subsequent meetings with Alcott and Emerson. See, for example, *A Writer of Books,* 427-431.

[85] *Ibid.,* 332.

[86] *Ibid.,* 332-333.

[87] *Ibid.,* 333.

[88] *Ibid.,* 333.

[89] *Letters of Emerson,* V, 521.

[90] *Ibid.,* V, 500; *Daily Missouri Democrat,* March 6, 1867.

[91] *Letters of Emerson,* V, 514. Emerson was in St. Louis on two subsequent occasions, on at least one of which he spoke to the Philosophical Society. See *Ibid.,* V, 456, n. 64; V, 514, n. 140; also V, 546.

[92] In the list of members as given by William Schuyler (*loc. cit.,* 72-73) eighteen individuals are listed as "directors," thirty-four as "associates," and forty-nine as "auxiliaries." All of the last-named lived at a distance from St. Louis, and included men like A. B.

Alcott, F. B. Sanborn, J. E. Cabot, D. A. Wasson, F. H. Hedge, and John Weiss of New England; J. B. Stallo and August Willich of Cincinnati; J. H. Stirling of Scotland and T. Collins Simon of England; A. Vera of Italy; José de Fonfriede of France; and Karl Rosenberg, Franz Hoffmann, Friedrich Kapp, Louis Feuerbach, Moritz Carriere, Jacob Bernays, and J. H. Fichte of Germany.

[93] *Letters of Emerson*, V, 521.

[94] *Ibid*, V, 458, 513-514, 521; VI, 15, 18-19, 103-104, 201, 210, 280, 284, 285-286.

[95] *Ibid.*, VI, 104.

[96] *Journal of Speculative Philosophy*, XV, iii (July, 1881), 303-320. (Hereafter referred to as *JoSP*.)

[97] *Journals of Emerson*, X, 475.

[98] There appears to be a good deal of confusion regarding whether the Philosophical Society grew out of the Kant Club or the Hegel Club, and whether the Kant Club is not the older of the two. The testimony is not conclusive, but what Harris specifically says in his preface to *Hegel's Logic* about his lectures before the Kant Club during 1877-1887 indicates that it outlived the Hegel Club, and that therefore it was the Hegel Club that became defunct in 1866 when it was merged with the newly organized Philosophical Society. See also D. H. Harris (ed.), *op. cit.*, 89-93, and William Schuyler, *loc. cit.*, 82-83.

[99] Charles M. Perry, *op. cit.*, 67.

[100] D. H. Harris (ed.), *op. cit.*, 17. Snider himself always maintained that it was less an off-shoot of New England Transcendentalism than a culmination of idealism in America, that it was never cliquish, partial, or provincial, but continental in its aim.

[101] See, for example, J. M. Greenwood, *Dr. William Torrey Harris, Educator, Philosopher, and Scholar. Delivered before the Missouri State Teachers' Association at St. Louis, Mo., Dec. 28, 1909* (Kansas City, 1910), 13. One instance among many is Harris' visitation, twice annually during 1870-1874, to the normal school founded in 1867 by Joseph Baldwin at Kirksville, Mo.,— occasions on which Harris improved every opportunity to spread the Hegelian doctrine. Another early sphere of influence was in

the normal school at Terre Haute, Indiana, where, with the help of Harris, an Hegelian system of teacher-training was formulated.

[102] For a brief sketch of the rich cultural and institutional life of Jacksonville, see the excellent study by Paul Russell Anderson, "Hiram K. Jones and Philosophy in Jacksonville," *Journal of the Illinois State Historical Society*, XXXIII, iv (Dec., 1940), 478-520.

[103] Harris left Jacksonville about 1880 and became associated with Snider's Communal University in St. Louis, and soon after, Block moved to Chicago and became Snider's lieutenant in the Kindergarten and Communal University movement in that city.

[104] In 1892 when the Akademe held its last meeting, the cumulative roll of members contained 433 names.—Paul Russell Anderson, *loc. cit.*, 507-508.

[105] For an excellent study of the Quincy School, see Paul Russell Anderson, "Quincy, an Outpost of Philosophy," *Journal of the Illinois State Historical Society*, XXIV, i (March, 1941), 50-83. When Professor Anderson publishes his investigation of the Osceola group, we shall know more about Johnson and his colleagues.

[106] *Records of the American Akademe*, MSS. preserved in the Illinois College Library, 3, 25.

[107] *Memories and Studies* (New York, 1911), 81-82. James is obviously in error in dating these occurrences as early as 1872-1873, for the "two young men from Illinois" did not arrive in Cambridge until 1879.

[108] Snider, *St. Louis Movement*, 100.

[109] *Ibid.*, 123.

[110] *Ibid.*, 179. Snider side-stepped or resolutely refused every offer that might deflect him from his course, even when the promise of pecuniary gain or influence was great He would not accept any administrative responsibility or tie himself to any academic position; he was a talented and lovable man, but he had to be a free-lance litterateur; he would not submit to having his works edited and consequently had to publish them himself. See his account of his "self-publication" as related in *St. Louis Movement*, 479-486.

[111] See Snider's chapter on "University Brokmeyer" in *A Writer of Books*, 343-362.

[112] Snider, *St. Louis Movement*, 33.

[113] *Ibid.*, 236.

[114] D. H. Harris (ed.) *op. cit.*, 26, 59-66, 127; Paul R. Anderson, "Hiram K. Jones and Philosophy in Jacksonville," *loc. cit.*, 514; Cleon Forbes, *loc. cit.*, 610-611.

[115] See his essay by that title in *Memories and Studies*, 75-103.

[116] Sanborn and Harris, *op. cit.*, II, 507-508.

[117] D. H. Harris (ed.), *op. cit.*, 483.

[118] *Journals of Alcott*, 483.

[119] Sanborn and Harris, *op. cit.*, II, 532-533. For details regarding costs to students—tuition, board, etc.—see the announcements printed in the *JoSP*, XIV, i (Jan., 1880), 135-138.

[120] F. B. Sanborn (ed.), *The Genius and Character of Emerson. Lectures at the Concord School of Philosophy* (Boston, 1884), v.

[121] *Ibid.*, x; *JoSP*, XIV, i (Jan., 1880), 135; iii (July, 1880), 251.

[122] *JoSP*, XVII, ii (April, 1883), 213.

[123] *JoSP*, XIX, ii (April, 1885), 220.

[124] *JoSP*, XXI, i (Jan., 1887), 110. These data, taken from the detailed reports of the successive sessions as reported in the *JoSP*, show some variation from the summary report by Sanborn in *The Genius and Character of Emerson*, ix-xxii; the former are the more accurate. The *JoSP* appears to have been the best agency for publicity at the disposal of the Concord School.

[125] Sanborn, reporting the first session in the *JoSP*, XIV, i (Jan., 1880), 137, said, "The whole number of persons (students, invited guests, and visitors) who attended one or more sessions of the school was nearly four hundred, of whom about one-fourth were residents of Concord. Others came from New Hampshire, Massachusetts, Vermont, Rhode Island, Connecticut, New York, New Jersey, Pennsylvania, Virginia, North and South Carolina,

Louisiana, Kentucky, Missouri, Colorado, California, Illinois, Indiana, Ohio, Wisconsin, Michigan, and Minnesota. Twenty-eight course tickets were issued, of which twenty-seven were used; about twenty complimentary course-tickets, of which perhaps fifteen were used; and about eleven hundred and fifty single tickets were issued and used. [The rate was $3 for each of the courses of ten lectures, but each regular student was required to buy at least $10 worth of course-tickets for the term; or, if he preferred, he could enroll for all courses, regular and special, for $15. Tickets for single lectures were 50 cents each.] The average attendance of students was forty; of students and faculty about forty-five; but at Mr. Emerson's lecture one hundred and sixty were present, and at several of the other sessions more than seventy."

Records of attendance for subsequent years are not available. Snider was of the opinion that the school of 1881, the third, represented the best year, and that thereafter its course was downward; but beyond estimating that the average attendance for a lecture was 50 and that upwards of 2,000 individual persons came to Concord to attend the lectures during the nine schools that were held, he gives no further figures. In view of Snider's tendency to belittle the popularity and influence of the Concord School in comparison with his own Western schools, the figure may have been well over 2,000. See Snider, *St. Louis Movement*, 350-373, 521-522, 535.

[126] *Journals of Alcott*, 496-497.

[127] *Ibid.*, 497.

[128] *Ibid.*, 498.

[129] *Ibid.*, 498.

[130] Paul R. Anderson, "Hiram K. Johnson and Philosophy in Jacksonville," *loc. cit.*, 501.

[131] Lillian Whiting, *Boston Days: The City of Beautiful Ideals, Concord and Its Famous Authors* (Boston, 1902), 175.

[132] *Journals of Alcott*, 499.

[133] *Ibid.*, 500.

[134] *Ibid.*, 500.

[185] *Ibid.*, 499.

[186] *Ibid.*, 500.

[187] *Ibid.*, 502.

[188] *Ibid.*, 502.

[189] *Ibid.*, 505.

[140] *Ibid.*, 505, (Aug. 4, 1879). The next day Harris gave his last lecture, on "The Dialectic." Alcott made the following notation: "He has a crowded audience and sums up the propositions of his course. He has drawn fuller audiences than any other member of the Faculty and won the confidence and respect of all who have heard him."—*Ibid.*, 505-506.

[141] *Ibid.*, 510.

[142] *Ibid.*, 510.

[143] The program as given does not correspond exactly with that announced in the *JoSP* the preceding January (XIV, i, 138). Compare the prospectus with the program as printed in F. B. Sanborn (ed.), *The Genius and Character of Emerson*, xii-xiii, and especially with the more detailed "programme" in *JoSP*, XIV, ii (April, 1880), 251-253.

Besides the courses by the "major Professors" named above, odd lectures were given during the second year by Mrs. E. D. Cheney (two on "Art"), Mrs. Julia Ward Howe (one on "Modern Society"), John Albee (two on "Literary Art"), Dr. Elishu Mulford (two on "The Relations of Religion and Philosophy to Christianity"), Professor Andrew P. Peabody (one on "Conscience and Consciousness"), and one each by Benjamin Peirce, C. A. Bartol, R. W. Emerson, F. H. Hedge, G. W. Howison, and John Wasson. Blake, as was customary, read from Thoreau's manuscripts.

[144] *JoSP*, XV, i (Jan., 1881), 76-77; iii (July, 1881), 303, 307.

[145] *JoSP*, XV, iii (July, 1881), 303-305.

[146] Snider, *St. Louis Movement*, 282.

[147] *JoSP*, XV, iii (July, 1881), 305.

[148] *Ibid.*, 305.

[149] *Journals of Alcott*, 497, 536.

[150] *JoSP*, XV, iii (July, 1881), 306.

[151] *Ibid.*, 306-307.

[152] Harris has been in touch with Morris since 1874, and more intimately after 1877 when Morris went to Johns Hopkins. The *JoSP* reported on his courses of lectures on German philosophy in both Baltimore and Ann Arbor, printed reviews of his publications, and published several of his original contributions to philosophy.

[153] *JoSP*, XV, iii (July, 1881), 307-311.

[154] *Ibid.*, 311.

[155] *Ibid.*, 311-312.

[156] *Ibid.*, 312.

[157] *Ibid.*, 312-313.

[158] *Ibid.*, 312-313.

[159] *Ibid.*, 314.

[160] *Ibid.*, 314-316.

[161] *Ibid.*, 316.

[162] *Ibid.*, 317.

[163] *Ibid.*, 317-319.

[164] *Ibid.*, 319-320.

[165] *Ibid.*, 320.

[166] The Concordians missed, by precisely one month, the honor of being the first to hold a Kant celebration in America. Professor John W. Mears of Hamilton College was responsible for arranging the first Kant centennial, observed in the parlor of the Temple Grove Hotel at Saratoga, N. Y., on July 6-7. According to the "Proceedings" prepared chiefly by the Secretary, Mr. W. C. Taylor, and published in the *JoSP* for July, 1881 (XV, iii, 293-302), those present were "President [Julius H.] Seelye, of Amherst College, who was chosen chairman; President Bascom, of Wisconsin University; Professors Morris, of Johns Hopkins University; Mears, of Hamilton College; Bennett, of Syracuse University; Bliss of

Vermont University; and S. A. Lyman, of Yale College; also Dr. Herrick Johnson and lady, of Chicago; Mr. Libbey, of the 'Princeton Review'; Mr. Thomas H. Pease and lady, of New Haven; the Rev. C. E. Lindsey and lady, of New Rochelle; Mr. A. L. Blair, of Troy; Mr. E. M. Wheeler, of Dover, Delaware; Miss Eliza A. Youmans, of New York City; Messrs. A. C. White, Frank S. Williams, F. W. Palmer, and R. W. Hughes, of the graduating class of Hamilton College; Rev. C. F. Dowd, Rev. Dr. Stryker and Miss Stryker [and W. C. Taylor of Saratoga], with others from Saratoga and other places." (*Ibid.*, 293.)

The participants in the program, together with the titles of their papers, were as follows: (1) J. W. Mears, "Significance of the Centennial," (2) George S. Morris, "The Higher Problems of Philosophy," (3) President John Bascom, "Kant's Distinction between Speculative and Practical Reason," (4) Josiah Royce, "A Critique of the *Critique*," read in part by F. S. Williams and in part by A. C. White, (5) Lester F. Ward, of the U. S. Geological Survey, "The Antinomies of Kant in Relation to Modern Science," read by R. W. Hughes, and (6) W. T. Harris, "The Relations of Kant's Kritik to Ancient and Modern Thought," read by Dr. Mears. The discussion provoked by the papers was no less lively than at Concord.

The report reproduced, also, twenty-five letters elicited by the occasion from prominent professors, theologians, and other representative men. These letters were almost without exception congratulatory of the noble purposefulness of the committee in arranging the commemorative exercise or adulatory in praise of Kant. Only two of the letters were negative in spirit. Professor B. N. Martin of New York University felt that "the incompleteness of his [Kant's] work forms so great a drawback upon its usefulness" that he "could never refer to it with enthusiasm" (*ibid.*, 299-300); while the great McCosh, pleading a previous engagement, regretted his inability to show his "reverence for Kant and his philosophy by attending the celebration," and closed with the profundity: "You know that I hold the opinion that the American student should labor to take from Kant all that is natural and true, and reject all that is artificial and false." (*Ibid.*, 302.)

one hundred forty

[167] *Journals of Alcott*, 518, 525.

[168] F. B. Sanborn (ed.), *The Genius and Character of Emerson*, xv-xvi. Other individual lectures included "Childhood," by E. P. Peabody, "Poetry," by John Albee, "Nature," by Mrs. E. D. Cheney, "Idols and Iconoclasts," by Julia Ward Howe, "The Symbolism of Color," by G. P. Lathrop, and a reading from Thoreau's manuscript by Sanborn.—*Ibid.*, xvi-xviii.

Several of the lectures of the fourth school (1882) were reproduced and others abstracted in an "unofficial" but "authorized" publication prepared by R. L. Brightman, "one of the journalists" who reported the Concord School, under the title, *The Concord Lectures on Philosophy* (Cambridge, Mass., 1883). See F. B. Sanborn (ed.), *The Genius and Character of Emerson*, v; and *JoSP*, XVII, iii (July, 1883), 317.

[169] *Journals of Alcott*, 432.

[170] Snider, *St. Louis Movement*, 307-308.

[171] To this group of "philosophical" lectures are to be added the "special" lectures (one each) by C. A. Bartol on "Optimism and Pessimism," Wasson on "Herbert Spencer's Casual Law of Evolution," Lewis J. Block on "Platonism and its Relation to Modern Thought," and Noah Porter on "Kant's Categorical Imperative." —*JoSP*, XVII, ii (April, 1883), 214-215; F. B. Sanborn (ed.), *The Genius and Character of Emerson*, xviii.

[172] F. B. Sanborn (ed.), *The Genius and Character of Emerson*, xviii; *JoSP*, XVII, ii (April, 1883), 214-215; *ibid.*, XVII, iii (July, 1883), 317-322.

[173] Snider, *St. Louis Movement*, 307-308.

[174] *Ibid.*, 307-308.

[175] *Ibid.*, 308.

[176] In addition to the fourteen lectures on Emerson, there were five (by A. P. Peabody, John Fiske, R. A. Holland, Thomas Davidson, and W. T. Harris) on Immortality. The lectures on Emerson can be conveniently turned to in Sanborn's edition of them under the title *The Genius and Character of Emerson*.

[177] For details, see *JoSP*, XIX, ii (April, 1885), 220-221; F. B. Sanborn (ed.), *op. cit.*, xx; and especially Sanborn's edition of *The Life and Character of Goethe. Lectures at the Concord School of Philosophy* (Boston, 1886), xxiii-xxiv.

[178] A similar volume which grew out of the Goethe School in Milwaukee, which Snider arranged there in 1886, affords interesting data for a comparison of East with West. See Marion V. Dudley (ed.), *Poetry and Philosophy of Goethe. Comprising the Lectures and Extempore Discussions before the Milwaukee Literary School in August, 1886,* Chicago, 1887. Unfortunately Brokmeyer's interesting, but very unexpected, remarks on *Faust* were not deemed canonical enough to bear publication.

[179] F. B. Sanborn (ed.), *The Genius and Character of Emerson,* xxi.

[180] *JoSP*, XX, iv (Oct., 1886), 426-443, and F. B. Sanborn (ed.), *The Life and Genius of Goethe,* v-xxiii.

[181] Snider, *St. Louis Movement,* 272-273, 274-275.

[182] He also manifestly enjoyed the story about the romantic young couple, walking in the Walden woods, who became so entangled in their discussion of the philosophy of love that the young lady explained to her suitor, "Pshaw! You are no philosopher, else you would understand the Yesⁿess of my No!" (*Ibid.,* 275.) In the same manner he related the jest of the young man who had picked up some bits of Hegelian nomenclature, and who made himself merry over the Concord Hegelians' definition of a hole in the coat as "the partial negation of the totality of being on-and-around-itself *(des an-und-um-sich Seyns)."* (*Ibid.,* 371.) Other choice quips are recorded by Austin Warren, *loc. cit.,* 207-208, 211-212.

[183] See, for example, Snider, *St. Louis Movement,* 277, 284, 307, 309-315, 327-338, 547-548.

[184] *Ibid.,* 286-289, 350-354.

[185] *Ibid.,* 277.

[186] *Ibid.,* 521-522.

[187] F. B. Sanborn (ed.), *The Life and Genius of Goethe,* xxv.

one hundred forty-two

[188] See *JoSP*, XX, iv (Oct., 1886), 426-443; i (Jan., 1887), 110-112, for the program which consisted of 12 lectures on Aristotle and 10 on Dramatic Poesy, including Aristotle's *Poetics*, the Dramatic Element in the Greek Drama and the Norse Edda, Aristophanes, Shakespeare, Marlowe, Ford and Massinger, Schiller, Browning, and two on general dramatic criticism.

[189] *JoSP*, XX, iv (Oct., 1886), 426-443.

[190] See Professor Merle Curti's well-considered analysis and appraisal of Harris in *Social Ideas of American Educators*. 310-347.

[191] Charles M. Perry, *op. cit.*, 52.

[192] *The Changes of a Quarter Century*, New York, 1929; quoted in *ibid.*, 52.

[193] *JoSP*, III, i (1869), v.

[194] Even while his personalism tended in the end to divert his Hegelianism into new channels, it is to be noted, as Professor Odell Shepard had observed (*Pedlar's Progress*, 484, 494-500) that the doctrine of personalism had been given some development as well as currency by both Alcott and the St. Louisans long before George H. Howison and Borden Parker Bowne gave it more precise development and application. But there is enough similarity between the "personal idealism" of Howison and Bowne, on the one hand, and Alcott's doctrine of Personality and the theories current among the St. Louis philosophers, on the other, to suggest more than a casual relationship. All agreed upon a doctrine which regards the ultimate reality of the world as incorporate in a Divine Person who "sustains the universe by a continuous act of creative will." (*Ibid.*, 494.) Thus they achieved a mediate position between the absolutism of Hegelian idealism and its antithetical philosophies of agnosticism, positivism, materialism, and naturalism. The various ramifications are as yet far from clear, but as investigation into the sources of personalism progresses, it is not improbable that what Whitman spoke of vaguely and Howison and Bowne more coherently as "Personalism" will be found to stem half from Alcott's doctrine of Personality, half from the theories developed among the St. Louis Hegelians. If that be true, we shall be able to point to another cyclic progression of thought and influence,

deriving basically from New England Transcendentalism, joining forces with elements of Western Hegelianism, given a new direction by Howison, eventually turning eastward, and, in individuals like Bowne, Royce, and even Creighton (each of whom had meanwhile drawn directly from sources in Germany), finding a new orientation and articulation in the East.

[195] Other contributors were John Dewey, C. C. Everett, Noah Porter, John Watson, J. S. Kedney, and W. T. Harris.

[196] *Principles of Philosophy,* in *Collected Papers* (6 vols., Cambridge, Mass., 1931-1935), I, 18, 42.

[197] Jean Wahl, *The Pluralist Philosophers of England and America* (London, 1925), 62, 192.

[198] *Letters of William James,* ed. by Henry James (2 vols., Boston, 1920), I, 94-95, 208, 265.

[199] Quoted from a manuscript letter, by Frances B. Harmon, *op. cit.,* 104.

[200] *Writings of Walt Whitman,* ed. by his Literary Executors (10 vols., New York, 1902), IV, 322; IX, 170.

[201] These relations cannot be detailed here. The entire story of how German philosophy entered and finally pervaded the American tradition remains untold. I hope to present it in outline in my more comprehensive study of German intellectual and literary influence in the United States, now completed and awaiting publication.